Spiritual

Queen

EMMA MUMFORD

This edition is published by
That Guy's House in 2018

www.ThatGuysHouse.com

hey,

Welcome to this wonderful book brought to you by That Guy's House Publishing.

At That Guy's House we believe in real and raw wellness books that inspire the reader from a place of authenticity and honesty.

This book has been carefully crafted by both the author and publisher with the intention that it will bring you a glimmer of hope, a rush of inspiration and sensation of inner peace.

It is our hope that you thoroughly enjoy this book and pass it onto friends who may also be in need of a glimpse into their own magnificence.

Have a wonderful day.

Love,

Sean Patrick

That Guy.

Praise For Emma Mumford

'Emma Mumford is devoted to leading, inspiring and encouraging women to step into who they truly are.'

Rebecca Campbell - Best-Selling Author of 'Light Is The New Black' & 'Rise Sister Rise'

-

'Emma Mumford has amazing energy - she'll go far!'

Yasmin Boland - Author of 'Moonology'

-

'Emma Mumford raises positive vibrations
of anyone who reads or follows her.
We're proud to have her as part of the
Soul & Spirit family'

Soul & Spirit Magazine

-

'There's an old expression about 'snatching victory from the jaws of defeat' – and Emma's story is a courageous and inspiring story of how she did just that… and how you can do the same. Get ready for some great insights on how to get from where you are to where you want to go.'

Brad Yates - Author and Speaker

Contents

This is for all of us, the dreamers, the believers working hard everywhere to share divine light into this world. Thank you to my love, friends and to my parents for always trusting my vision and helping me to expand and grow into the woman I am today. I want to thank the universe, my guides and Angels also for sending me on an awakening so that I could write this book and for always having my back. I love you all.

Part 1

My Journey

Introduction

It's 4th September 2017 and I'm writing the first pages of this book. As it currently stands I don't have a book deal or any interest in this book being published. No one even knows I'm writing this really. I feel guided. I feel this is the right time to share my message with the world and share with you exactly who I am and how I got here, so that you too can awaken and be unapologetically you. This book will help change your life and that's bloomin' exciting. Within these pages I will share with you my past, my struggles, everything that led me up to my spiritual awakening, what triggered me to live a fiercely authentic life and help so many others do the same too. This won't be some bullshit book that claims to change your life and then forces you to buy more content or wait for my second book. No, I'm giving you every ounce of my journey, the struggles and successes so that you can truly see what has led me to this point in my life, and why I chose this as my life path. This book has landed in your hands for a reason and darling it's no coincidence!

For the last year or so I've tried to get in every door to make this book happen. When I got invited to Penguin publishing to interview one of my spiritual idols Meik Wiking, I thought this is it…Sadly, whatever door I've knocked on so far, the book deal hasn't been on the other side. It was only while sat in Santorini on my first holiday with my Mr Right, transforming my life within Rebecca Campbell's 'Light Is The New Black' book that I realised. Emma you have manifested your dream man, dream house, dream holidays, Tony Robbins picking you out of a crowd of three thousand people AND hugging you. Girl you can manifest a book deal!

So this is what I'm doing. I'm not writing this book to deadlines, or even with an end goal. I am writing this entire book on faith, love, belief and the knowing that by the end I will have a book deal and you will be reading this. My message will be heard and the Universe will sort the rest for me.

I knew from a very young age that I would write books. It was just a knowing, something which has guided me through my entire life. How could an eight year old girl just know that her books would be in WHSmith one day and read by a lot of people?

I remember looking way up to the top shelf as I was actually quite small back then (surprisingly) and just thinking to myself 'My book will be there one day, and I will be well known for what I do'. Even at the tender age of eight I knew what was ahead of me, my little old soul was giving me 'spoilers' as I like to call them. I know some of my followers will be disappointed that this isn't a money-saving book, but I've known from day one it was never going to be about Couponing. I'm more than that, way more than that as I will explain later on. I wanted this book to be a life book, not an autobiography, hell I'm only twenty-five! I wanted you to be able to pick this up and feel inspired, awakened and have the knowing within yourself that if I can do it, so can you. I'm a normal girl from Dorset, who has failed many times, had her heart broken, hit rock bottom and risen fiercely from the ashes all within five years. The Universe gave me this journey to share with you. It's not a pretty story, it gets extremely ugly in places, but no matter what, everything had to happen for an incredible reason.

This book will be your guide, through your good days and your bad days. Just know that whenever you feel helpless this book is your hope. I will be your biggest cheerleader cheering you on to create the life of your dreams. This book goes further than simply the Law of Attraction. This book is what happens next and the lessons you learn after you realise - this is all much bigger than manifesting the dream man, money and success. The real lesson here is love in all forms and through learning all these lessons the hard way - I share with you the techniques, thoughts, and actions, spirit showed me in my own moments of helplessness. You have a rockin' spiritual team around you who are always supporting you, rooting for you and dancing all around you every time you overcome a spiritual hurdle. It's time to uncover them, learn from them and hear the divine loud and clear. When we live in a world full of illusion, I want you to be able to determine what's love and what's illusion.

Once you awaken you think...oh fab now I finally feel alive and can manifest my dreams! Yes you can, but darling that was just the first step. The Universe does send you back to school and this is a journey, a beautiful one full of re-discovery and magic. Once you awaken you clear all shadow and ego within you - which is a beautiful thing as you can finally be at peace and share even more light into the world. This book has changed so much since I started writing it, because the Universe has sent me on a journey of more self-discovery and life lessons. The beauty of this is, I'm able to channel more love into this book and I hope you can feel uplifted and deeply loved when you read this book.

So who am I? I am…Emma Mumford. A Life Coach, The Coupon Queen, a Girl Boss, an Author, a Spiritual Queen, a Healer, a YouTuber, a Blogger and a Law of Attraction Practitioner. You certainly couldn't fit all of that into a Twitter bio!

Business Queen

So what led me to becoming my own boss and running two limited companies all by the age of twenty-four? I knew from a very young age that I wanted to be a business owner. I remember watching a TV show called 'The Apprentice' with my parents and thinking I could do this!

I've always been a creative person and wanted to follow in my Dad's entrepreneurial footsteps. The only problem was I had no idea what product I would sell. When I was deciding on my GCSEs at school, YouTube, Blogging & Influencers didn't even exist. I remember one day in my business studies class, our teacher went round the class and asked us to create a presentation to launch our businesses. I never knew how to put into words what I felt I would do as a business. I knew I would be the product, that it would be successful and it would be online. So I tried as hard as possible to translate that into this presentation. When it got round to me standing up in front of the class, I simply remember my peers and teacher laughing at me. They said how on earth could I be the product and that basically I just wanted to be a celebrity. I felt hurt and humiliated by this. I knew with every ounce of my soul this is what I would do. Why did I need to make a product to run a business? Well for those of you who were in that class or even my teacher, if you're reading this, it wasn't such an impossible idea after all!

After working for my Dad's business on and off throughout my teenage years, I knew this was the path I wanted to follow. I had no idea how, when or what the hell I would do but once again I just had this belief the Universe would magically make it happen and everything was going to work out.

When I turned eighteen and lived with my first ex-boyfriend, I was working at a well-known bank by this point and just wanted more from life. I looked at my hobbies and what I was good at. 'Nails' kept coming up time and time again. I used to do my friends' nails all the time and had quite the talent for nail art. I decided to qualify as a nail technician. Within three weeks and £1,000 later, I was a qualified nail technician. I had no idea what I was doing, or how I'd get clients but I had a full-time job so this was really just an experiment. I started 'Hard as Nails' back in 2013, because of my competitive prices and due to being extremely good at getting stock ridiculously cheaper than anyone else, other nail technicians in the area hated me! I had so much drama thrown at me from other technicians because I was under cutting them. Well I was thrifty even back then! I grew a good client base very quickly and everyone was always so impressed with the quality and standard. I even had other technicians book in with me to test out what all the fuss was about. I felt rather honoured they cared so much! Eventually after my business name was dragged through the mud by jealous technicians, I had to change the name to Perfect Ten Boutique which I much preferred anyway, definitely sounded a bit classier! I carried on this business in my spare time for another six months, but had to give it up when I became ill with anxiety and depression and eventually left my job at the bank. It left a lot of my clients gutted and the haters satisfied that I had been stopped finally. I still get messages now asking if I still do nails. It really does show how quickly I made an impact where I lived.

After that venture I felt deflated. I had to go and work at a clothes shop part-time and felt dulled down once again by working for someone else. On the 10th September 2013 my life would change forever as I created the Facebook page 'Extreme Couponing and Deals UK'. At this time I was still with my first ex-boyfriend and we were in a difficult position financially. I had to quit my job at the clothes shop and couldn't work due to not being able to even leave the house, due to anxiety. Money was tight and I had taken on his £7,000 debt. I wanted to help us out, and one day saw the American TLC show 'Extreme Couponing' on TV and knew I was on to something. I started looking online to see whether anyone in the UK did this so I could save money. There was only one person at the time doing this. There wasn't much information online, so I decided to start looking myself. After a few weeks I had filled my entire spare room with my stock pile of products exactly like how you see them on the show. My friends and family were baffled yet amazed at how I had gained over £300 worth of food and cleaning products for less than £50. My house did look like a supermarket though. My friends then pestered me to start a Facebook page to share my knowledge and to help others and that is how my business was born!

Within the first few months I'd received over 10,000 Facebook likes. By Christmas 2013 the press started getting involved as I was doing £1,000 shops for as little as £3! Couponing saved me really. I couldn't leave the house but these little bits of paper forced me to leave, to go to the shop and save money. It became an obsession. One that got me out of a really dark stage in my life. It gave me confidence and a great satisfaction that I was helping people better their own lives. So after being splashed across most newspapers over the Christmas period with my bargain Christmas haul, I was nicknamed The Coupon Queen and that's how she was born!

I then went on to do various TV appearances, numerous magazine articles and radio appearances. It really was surreal how within four months of starting this Facebook page, which I literally thought three people would read, it had nearly 100,000 followers and I was on national TV. It felt natural, it felt right to help people. I had no idea that what I had created would become what it is today, let alone a profitable business. This is how I met my first Guardian Angel.

About a year after I started this Facebook page, I got a message from a gentleman in the page's inbox. It simply read "Why aren't you earning off this page Emma?" Up until this point I had done all of this work every single day 100% unpaid. Confused, I replied but thought to myself, could this be a scammer? The man explained that I could earn money through affiliates. He invited me to join his Facebook group where he used affiliate links and dedicated an evening to show me how to use them, what networks to sign up to and answered all of my questions. I couldn't believe how kind this man was. Without him, I would have never of earned any money and been able to fulfil my dreams of being self-employed. A week later I remember going to message him as I'd made £100 already. I wanted to thank him for all of his help but his profile had been deleted. I then searched for his Facebook group and this too had been deleted. Every single trace of him online had vanished just like that! Baffled I thought to myself was he even real? Wherever you are thank you, but I'm certain this was an angel sent to help me along my path.

From that point on, within one month I was earning more than I'd ever earned in employment and since that day three years ago my business has gone from strength to strength. Two years ago after brands were pestering me to start writing reviews for their products and share them with my followers, I started my blog The Coupon Queen.

Since then I've turned it into a separate venture to Extreme Couponing and Deals UK. It's a beauty, lifestyle and travel blog which has more of my personality and personal life on it and has even won awards! I also now have my own YouTube channel which has over 26,000 subscribers and again covers much of the same and of course the law of attraction and spirituality! YouTube was extremely hard to crack and I'll be honest, I hated filming money-saving videos, it just wasn't me anymore. So I started to film beauty and fashion videos which at first got an awful response because I was The Coupon Queen. Two years on from the rebrand, my YouTube channel is growing at a rapid pace and it's all since I started covering Spirituality! I found my calling, something I could literally talk about for hours and hours. My most viewed video at this point is how I manifested my dream man, which is a 45 minute long video and has over 75,000 views. You might want to make a cup of tea before you sit down and watch that one! I will cover this topic in a later chapter anyway as I actually missed a lot out of that video without realising, it's a very big topic!

Running my own businesses has been extremely rewarding and has certainly made me grow as a person. I get to do incredible things every single day of my life. I have my own candle range, I get to present on This Morning, I get to go to London to really cool Blogging events and even meet celebrities. Really, I'm living the dream but it's not all been smooth sailing.

I've been extremely blessed in the fact I've never had any financial issues when starting my businesses. I started my business with £0 in my bank and absolutely no investment and have since grown these into two successful limited companies. With this success though comes the haters. In every walk of life you're going to have competitors or people who want to bring you down. Sadly, mine's a little more public than I would have liked. Since starting my couponing business, I've always had followers who didn't support what I did. When I started appearing in the press, they would say I was selfish and write hate comments because of how much money I'd saved. It was all pathetic behaviour really as I was trying to spread the message of coupons to help people. I've even had hate pages set up about me where these people would all go and fester in the mutual negativity. Not exactly what I'd call a productive use of their time. Why me? What had I done to these people? Having to read these comments on my hard work did hurt, and I've had to grow a thick skin, certainly in this line of work. Just because I'm a public figure does not mean I am public property.

The worst hate has actually come from other money-savers in the community. I'm not going to sit here and list examples or names, because we're all here to do the same job; help people save money. Honestly, I have never known such a negative and immature community like it. Trust me, I had enough warning about the blogging community but they haven't got anything on what these money-savers do. I think the reason I've kept myself to myself and my business close to my chest is because of these people. It's sad that I can't trust anyone in that industry anymore and that they'd want to bring people down like this. I've seen and heard some awful things these people have done to other money saving Facebook pages. It's just sad, really sad that these people are spouses, parents and all of them older than myself. Yet they have to bring down a girl just trying to do some good in the world.

I think this behaviour is what showed me that I'd never be in money-saving forever. It's been an incredible stepping stone. It has brought me incredible joy and amazing opportunities which I am forever grateful for. I'm currently selling that business to a dear friend of mine and know this feels good now. I trust he will run my baby well and make it even more of a success. I love that on my blog and YouTube channel I can be myself more and share with you my experiences and what I'm passionate about. I could never do that on my couponing page because of how people judged me. They didn't want to know Emma, they just wanted to save money.

Being a girl boss from such a young age has certainly brought challenges. I was twenty when I started and had absolutely no idea what I was doing. If I'm honest I'm still winging it now. Many find that hard to believe and almost insulting that I'm still winging it. Yes I have goals, I have ideas of what I want to achieve but I don't have a five-year strategy, I don't have some business manager planning my every move. It's still just me, following my intuition and doing what I want to do every single day. I do find it weird travelling up to London for board meetings and especially in my money-saving work being surrounded by corporate men. I find when working with companies and affiliates I often deal with men, which of course I don't mind but some of them seem to mind a lot that they have to deal with a young female entrepreneur. It's sad that people like that are still living in the past. It's tough making it in a man's world, but with the rise of the divine feminine upon us, it certainly won't be like this forever as more females awaken and rise up to share their message with the world. More and more of us are becoming incredible girl bosses and it's heart warming to witness. Why can't we all just root for one another and want others to succeed too regardless of gender?

Throughout my career I've always helped others. I've helped competitors in their early days and have been burnt when they had taken all the knowledge they needed off me. This has happened in the money-saving community, blogging community, even YouTube. I'll always help anyone, that's my nature; I was born to help people. Helping people doesn't detract anything away from my brands, my success or my values. There is enough success to go around and the way we rise up is by lifting others with us. So no, I don't regret helping any of these people out, because no matter what I'll always help people.

One of the many things I love about what I do now is all the wonderful messages you send me day in day out. I make a big effort to reply to every single one of them as you've taken the time out of your day to watch my videos and support me, so I want to reply to your messages and thank you directly. It is becoming increasingly more difficult as more and more of you are doing it, but every single comment, email and message fills me up with so much gratitude, love and positivity. Hearing how my videos and advice has helped you in your own lives fills me with so much happiness and joy. I think my favourite story that will stick with me forever more, was from a lady who commented on one of my YouTube videos. She explained about how her and her husband had been trying for a baby for some time with no success. With all hope lost she turned to the law of attraction and found my videos. After watching several of them she followed the advice I gave, and within a month they got pregnant! So now because of my work a new soul has been brought into this world and made this couple's dream come true. I can't even find the words to describe how this makes me feel. My work is making a huge difference in people's lives and that's all I've ever wanted.

So I've spoken about my couponing business and The Coupon Queen blog. My other business is Law of Attraction based. A part of it being my Blog shop and Etsy store which I launched last year. My store sells merchandise, planners, prints and courses. I have never felt I was particularly gifted in the graphic design department, but over the last year or so after being let down, I have self-taught myself to create these products and found a real passion for it. I love having positive quotes and products around my house to uplift and inspire all those who visit me. I really do take pride in my home as I'm there a lot of the time being self-employed. Everyone who's spent time in my home says how positive it always feels and how they always leave feeling uplifted. I will cover how I do this later on. I didn't really expect much from my merchandise venture, it was a little side project I wanted to do and it's actually going really well. It runs itself now really and I enjoy shipping all of your orders!

My new business incorporates my own name, Emma Mumford LTD. This covers my Law of Attraction work, life coaching and self-development courses. As it stands, I currently have a blogging course called 'Start Blogging Your Way To Success' and a 'Law of Attraction Development Guide'. You can find these in the shop section of my blog. I decided to start doing courses as so many of you kept asking for advice and how exactly I've done all of this! It covers a wide variety of topics and is designed to give you everything you need to start a successful blog and get great results. I've even included my top contacts to help get you started. It has been greatly received and I have more courses on the way! I started secretly doing life coaching sessions around a year ago now. I didn't really announce that I was doing them as I wanted to start off slowly due to demand from my other businesses. I still don't really promote it enough, but thoroughly enjoy the regular clients I do have. It's great to meet new people willing to change their lives and I take great pride in helping them transform and manifest their heart's desires. I cover all things from relationships, Law of Attraction and business coaching; you name it I do it! I think life coaching, blogging and my YouTube channel have to be my favourite parts of my businesses, simply because I get to enjoy helping people and interacting with you.

Crazily, I still run everything by myself! I genuinely can't tell you how I do it. Although I am manifesting the dream employee as it's getting to point where I do need to take someone on so I can free up some of my time. I want to settle down and when I have a family actually spend time with them. It's important for me to work hard now so that I can re-evaluate and re-focus on the right things that set my soul alight once I have a family. Who knows what the future holds with my businesses. I certainly see myself being self-employed throughout my life. I see myself going from strength to strength and moving on from money-saving fully. It will always be a part of me, I love getting a bargain don't get me wrong but my soul is calling and I really see myself writing more books and inspiring people. I'd love to one day travel the world and meet as many of you as possible. Hold events, reach out to even more people and help them to live an incredible life. I better get that on my manifestation board!

If I've learnt anything from being a girl boss over the last five years, it's that you should never let anyone tell you your worth. If I'd listened to all the haters, the critics, to my competitors and let them win, god I'd be depriving this world of so much! Imagine if I listened to them all those years ago, you wouldn't be reading this book that's for sure. So my advice to you would be, all negativity and hate stems from jealousy. Any negative emotion from someone else is not a reflection of you, it's a reflection from inside them. Whenever I receive any negativity now, I simply read it and send the person love and healing. Clearly, something must be troubling them that much, that they feel the need to project it onto a stranger like me. So I simply send them love and delete it. It certainly sounds like I've had a whirlwind success and I guess I have over the last five years. That doesn't mean I haven't sat exactly where you are now like, shit can I really do this? I wouldn't be human if I didn't doubt myself sometimes.

A lot of people are under the illusion that I have a whole team of people helping me behind the scenes. I love that people think this because clearly I'm doing something right, but I can assure you it's still just little old me sat behind the computer screen day in day out working my arse off. I don't get days off and I even work on Christmas Day. My friends are baffled why I dedicate every single day of my life to my work, but it's because it's my passion it never really feels like work. Most days I can do my work and be done by midday so I'm free to go out with my friends, see my family and live life on my own terms. Yes, I am tied to my businesses and it does mean that even if I go away on holiday I have to work, but it's easy and I do it. So for now it's the perfect solution. I know in the future things will be different, and I will need to take on help but that's the next step in my girl boss journey, allowing someone into my business and actually delegating them tasks. The key in business is to turn your fear into fuel. I did this by saying yes to everything, it may sound silly but it bloody works.

I started saying yes to everything and worrying about how I'd do it all later. When This Morning approached me about a regular money-saving slot on their show, did I know what it entailed? No! Was I prepared? No! Had I done live TV before? Hell no! On the 3rd October 2016 I just rocked on up to the ITV studios and bloomin' winged it like always. I had obviously prepared the deals and coupons that I spoke about live on air, but I had no idea whether I could do this, whether I would be any good, only the Universe knew that one and luckily I was good. I'm really bad at over committing myself. I'm not happy and on top form unless I'm working on several projects at once. Even now writing this I know I have several deadlines approaching and I really should be getting on with them, but I enjoy this too much. This is my passion. One day I'll learn and employ someone!

I think the secret if anything to becoming a successful girl boss is being authentic. There are so many people in this world living a fake life (hell I was!). There are too many copies and not enough crazy, ambitious, authentic girl bosses out there. We live in a Universe where anything is possible, and now thanks to technology we can create businesses out of absolutely anything! Stop helping fulfil someone else's dream. This is your time to shine - you can start making an inspiring story and your business today. If I can make an award-winning limited company out of coupons, you can do anything you put your mind to!

"It is in your moments of decision
that your destiny is shaped."

—Tony Robbins

Independent Queen

So this is where the story takes a negative turn. Many of my friends and family don't know the true extent of these relationships or just how crippling they really were. I'd had boyfriends throughout school and reluctantly lost my virginity at the age of sixteen. I honestly don't remember it happening. Sorry Mum, I am going to talk about sex. I wish looking back I'd have waited. Boys can be so deceiving when they're young, telling you how much they love you just to get you into bed. I was in a relationship when it happened, but after him leaving me, for what honestly was a downgrade, the very next week, it hurt me a lot. God, I really have been with some awful boyfriends I honestly don't know what I was thinking looking back! Next up was the druggie, who could never get it up because of the amount of horse tranquilliser he used to take to get a high. I mean you couldn't even make it up! I do laugh at that whole situation now and how much shit I tolerated from this guy. We were eighteen at the time, young, immature and drugs were the 'in thing'. They never appealed to me personally and I never ended up trying them. I was just so different to everyone around me back then. After the druggie I was single for a year. This marked the start of my five year cycle which would change my life forever.

I met my first ex-boyfriend when I was working at a phone shop. We worked together and we had a spark straight away. I thought he was good looking and he had tattoos, so really I was sold already. We started dating and he was actually quite romantic in the beginning. I don't remember the sex being anything special. I don't even remember it at all so it couldn't have been that mind blowing! I don't remember ever saying that I loved him, I don't think I ever truly felt love with him. We moved into our house after six months of being together, a little rushed maybe but it did feel right at the time. We lived near his parents in probably the most run down part of our hometown, again certainly not where I wanted to be. This started the long list of sacrifices I made for these guys and settling for way less than I deserved. After a year of being together the cracks started to show, it felt so loveless and shit. I've known from a very young age that I was born to be a mother and a wife, it's all I've ever dreamed of. Yet not once did I ever discuss kids or marriage with him. It felt like I shut all of this out of my life for him. I felt emotionless but wanted to stay with him for some unknown reason. We started getting knocks at the door from bailiffs demanding money. This is when I truly learnt who he was as a person. Within three months we must have had over seven bailiffs turn up, all when he was at work so I had to deal with them. To my knowledge at that time he owed around £8,000 to various creditors. I was working at a well known bank by this time and sat him down to discuss his options. He explained how the debt was from a previous girlfriend who had screwed him over and created this elaborate story of her wrong doing. Feeling sorry for him, the very next day I went to work and took out a £7,000 loan in my own name to clear his debts. My manager knew it was for him and should never have given me that loan in the first place. He was a father himself. It angers me that he didn't see what was happening. Looking back it all had to happen like this to have everything beautiful I have today. So I paid off his debts and he was grateful that I had done this. He started repaying the loan each month and I felt like I'd taken a big weight off our relationship.

After a few months he stopped making the loan repayments which resulted in me getting two defaults on my credit file. Our relationship deteriorated very quickly and my emotionless feelings for him turned into hate very quickly. We split up for a week and I moved back home to my parents. By that point more debt had come through the door. It must have been up to £30,000 by this point and he just kept lying. His family were awful with money and would actively tell him ways to avoid all of this debt like they were speaking from experience. They were nice enough but their values were all wrong. I hated being around people with no life goals or any motivation whatsoever. In the week we spent apart I remember feeling so shit that I was back at my parents house. I had no freedom, no independence anymore, I needed to get out. I remember writing a list of pros and cons of our relationship and decided to go back there because I'd lose my independence and my friends. I made the decision selfishly and didn't even care about him. That was the problem; we were more like flat mates. We didn't kiss, we didn't do anything, he was more like a friend. So after moving back in things just got worse and worse. I found out the debt was due to gambling and I actually contacted his ex to find out the debt she left him in actually was all bullshit! He had a shopping addiction and used all these credit facilities to buy tons of unnecessary things. All of this made sense as I had witnessed these qualities in him, but wait for it…I still didn't leave him for another six months!

At this point I knew I was leaving. I had to make a plan
of how to get out and get my £7,000 back. My first ex got
very angry and bitter towards the end of our relationship.
I bought him a beautiful pug puppy named Max for his
birthday, and I really enjoyed bringing him up for the
twelve weeks I was there. Max felt like my only friend at
some points in that house. My ex used to smash things and
be violent and Max would always run straight to me as he
knew I'd never let anything happen to him. I remember him
shaking and crying in fear. I never should have left Max
with him but I had to get myself out of there in one piece
first. By this point I was heavily depressed, I couldn't even
leave the house. I had to leave work because I couldn't face
anyone anymore. I was a wreck, constantly having panic
attacks. Throughout all of this I started my couponing
business. How I'll never know. It honestly felt like that
business saved my life sometimes.

In walked ex number two who was a massive help in leaving!
I needed a saviour and he certainly seemed like it. I felt a
bond very quickly to him and at this point I was still with
my first ex. I wasn't cheating, but looking back I shouldn't
have even been talking to him. I should have left my current
situation and sorted myself out first. My second ex was
certainly the charmer and knew all of the right things to say
at the right time. On the 22nd December 2013 (great timing
Emma), I decided to walk away for good. My best friend
Annie was over and my first ex had left his phone in the
bathroom. I knew something was going on with him, just as
he knew I'd met someone else.

I grabbed his phone and locked Annie and I in the bathroom. Within seconds we had found all the proof we needed to see. Pictures, sexts, the whole bloody lot! I didn't feel so guilty for simply talking to someone now. In that moment I didn't feel anger nor hate, nothing like that. I felt peace and that I finally had everything I needed to leave this life behind me. Annie and I went out that evening into town for some drinks and we planned how I'd leave him, she has seriously been my rock throughout the last five years. Without Annie I don't think I ever would have been strong in both of these situations. I remember going back that night and for what must have been two hours, I sat and just talked at him. I still to this day couldn't tell you what I said to him but it was a break up speech. It didn't matter, I was leaving. All through the night I packed, I was done. I text my Dad to come and pick me up in the morning. I think my parents were delighted that I had finally seen the light. In the morning I'd packed up my entire life on no sleep. I went upstairs to say goodbye to Max more than anything, and my ex was shocked, he thought I'd been joking. I remember holding Max and breaking down, I couldn't leave him here but he wasn't mine. I looked into his innocent eyes and just thinking please God protect him. My parents picked me up and we crammed as much as we could into my Dad's car. It was over now, I could be free.

Following the break up, he made it extremely clear he would not be paying the £7,000 back to me. To this day he has never made a single payment and has avoided all legal correspondence. Even recently I had a bailiff letter come through to my new home for him. It was easy to sort but I thought to myself I really hope one day he changes. I could have taken him to court. I had enough proof of absolutely everything but I was a mess, I needed to focus on me and getting myself better. After three years of saving and becoming self-employed I paid off the £7,000 myself. It was hard and there were days I used to think what the hell am I doing this for? Now I see just how much I gained from that relationship. I may have lost £7,000 but the Universe has paid me it back and way more since starting my businesses. It is because of him I have my businesses, my success and this incredible life now. Thank you for doing all of this, because of you I am happy and have a life I never dreamed possible. I felt like I'd hit rock bottom in that relationship, boy was I in for a shock with the next one...

After leaving my first ex, instead of sitting back and thinking I need to sort my own life out first, I stupidly went into my next relationship three days later on Christmas day. Not one of my best decisions I'll admit. My second ex was very caring and kind in the beginning. A lot of shit to do with the first ex surfaced for many months afterwards so he had to tolerate a lot of that. I also started getting CBT (Cognitive Behavioural Therapy) for my anxiety and depression. I can't tell you what attracted me to my second ex. Looking back I didn't fancy him, he wasn't what I wanted at all. He was shorter than me, three years younger than me, over weight and I think he was just there at the right time and because of that, I felt he was the one. We spoke about marriage and kids very early on and we did fall very quickly for one another. If I compare this feeling to what I have now, I'll be honest I don't know

whether it was love. I think it was lust. The Buddhists say
if you meet somebody and your heart pounds, your hands
shake and your knees go weak, that's not the one. When you
meet your soulmate you'll feel calm. No anxiety or agitation,
just peace at last. I certainly did not feel calm around him. I
felt anxious. I felt like I needed to be someone else for him
and so I became that person. Our relationship was doomed
from the get go really. I wasn't myself. I was living a huge
lie once again about who I was. His parents didn't like me
because I was successful by this point, independent, and I
stood up for myself sometimes. I was slowly getting stronger.
His family liked to think they were the mafia, claiming to
have killed people and being bad arses. Trust me, all talk!
They liked to blame their misfortunes in life always on other
people, nothing was ever their own fault and they were all
certainly living in victim mode. I used to hate being around
them. Even spending Christmas with them, it was always
so negative and all fake. After two years of being together I
decided I wanted to move out of my parents' house and into
a place with him. Well he certainly wasn't having this. He
couldn't possibly leave his beloved parents. It turned into
numerous arguments and even his parents verbally attacking
me. In the end his mother finally gave her sacred blessing and
all of a sudden like magic he wanted us to move in together!

My Dad kept saying to me, "Emma don't do this. He doesn't
want to live with you", but I wouldn't listen. I was determined
to give myself the happily ever after I deserved. Looking
back I see how wrong all of this was. Nothing should be
forced and seeing how naturally things are progressing with

Mr Right now it is true what they say. When it's right it just happens naturally. We eventually found a top floor flat in my dream town, Poundbury. Things started deteriorating very quickly. A year before we split up, I'm certain the cheating started. He started going to the gym with her, which at first I didn't mind but my gut knew and I started to panic. I was jealous and I was angry because I knew what was happening. He wasn't losing weight or toning up. He made me feel crazy, like I was imagining the whole thing. He was extremely manipulative and clever with how he used me, and had me right where he wanted me. You'll notice I haven't mentioned sex yet, I'll get to that. Our relationship was a weird one. It was certainly intense and there was a strong soul connection, I know that for sure. I could never explain it, he was a soulmate just not my forever person. He always had such a hold on me. I pushed away my friends and family. I'd have done anything for him and I did.

I find the words hard to get out. I've never spoken about these experiences let alone written the words. He started to get angry towards the end of our relationship. I didn't help things as I would want to piss him off and hurt him like he was hurting me. I thought this was love. I thought this was how happily ever after was meant to be. I remember one day things got really bad. I was in my office working and he came home from work. We broke into the 176th row of the week, and he started to throw my things around. Naturally defending my work and possessions, I pushed him away and closed the door. He started to get more and more violent, punching and kicking the door as I pushed with all of my strength to keep it closed and him away from me. In that moment I thought, if he gets this door down what am I going to do? I genuinely feared for my safety. I couldn't let this happen. I prayed in that moment for the first time in years. Eventually, as I didn't want my landlord to evict us due to kicking doors down, I gave up. He grabbed me and as I was screaming for him to let me go I didn't recognise him anymore. I looked into his eyes begging for him to stop and I saw nothing but an empty soul. After grabbing me, he realised he had hurt me and stopped. What happened next was humiliating, soul destroying and something I've shut out of my mind for over a year now.

Sex with him was never love, it was sex. I would say I've always been very reserved and have always been shy with all of my boyfriends. I'm not very confident at all in that department and it's no surprise with my history. There's certain things I've never wanted to do and never felt comfortable with, but that wasn't good enough for him. He never respected my values or my modesty. He used to say that I was a shit girlfriend because I wouldn't do certain things and he would constantly make me feel worthless and ugly. Many things happened nonconsensual from that moment on, I just let him do everything he wanted to me. Why wasn't I fighting back? Truthfully, I thought this was love. I didn't know any different. Boys had treated me like this all of my life. Maybe I just had high expectations? I didn't say anything. I didn't do anything. I don't even remember thoughts coming into my mind. I just remember blankness. I remember feeling disgusting, sick and empty afterwards. This was the moment

I wanted my life to end. What happened still affects me to this day. I've dealt with it in my own way. There are still things I don't feel comfortable doing now, simply because it brings all these horrible emotions back up. It's hard to just erase all of this from my memory. Sometimes I question why the Universe would let this happen to me. Equally I felt that I should have been strong enough to deal with this at the time and walk away.

After that day it was never the same again. Really this whole situation was fucked up, it certainly fucked my mind royally. I spiralled into a heavy and disturbing depression. Some days I wouldn't get out of bed. Shamefully, one day when I was certain I was going to end my life, I lay in bed holding a knife for sixteen hours solid. No food, nothing. I just stared into space wishing the pain would end. Now for those who know me well, this must sound like I'm talking about a completely different person. I am really. This wasn't me, it never was. There was an imposter in my head. My soul was so broken and lost I never thought I'd see the light again.

The week we split up was a turbulent one. He decided he wanted to leave, but I had nothing or no one. I couldn't let this happen. He was like oxygen to me. Without him I felt I would have died. This is completely unhealthy and now I'm free from this I realise just how wrong everything was, I never deserved any of this. I begged him to stay and he did. For the next few days we tried to make this frankly pile of shit relationship work. It's almost laughable at how hard I tried to make myself worthy for him. Each night he was going out to see her and came home in the early hours of the morning acting like we were fabulous. I remember on his birthday he didn't invite me out with his friends he demanded I stayed at home so he could see her. He said he'd be back by 2am. I woke up at 3am worrying; no texts, nothing so I called him; no response. I just wanted to know he was okay. I sat by the window crying for what must have been two hours solid. Begging God to help me, I just kept saying help me please! This is the first time I felt heard. The Universe knew I was ready at this point and started the process of awakening. He never did come home that night. He stayed at his parents with her. With each passing day I grew stronger until 16th April 2016 I finally said no more. It was like someone had taken over my body. I wasn't aware of what I was saying or doing. These divine words just came out of my mouth. Something saved me that day. Whether it was my soul finally speaking up or my ego, I had ended things. I was free.

The next few weeks that followed were hard. My parents weren't very supportive and my friends at the time didn't care. I was alone and surrounded by shit and negativity. It was no surprise I was suicidal. I couldn't afford to go back to CBT now he was refusing to pay the rent. Basically, we had a rental agreement until the November and he agreed to pay it until then and be a 'gentleman' about things. I never saw a penny. The day he left he still owed me £3,000 for a TV he made me buy him on my credit facility and other expenses. I've never seen a penny of it. For the next four months he continued to lead me on, tell me he was coming back, that he loved me and that we just met too young. His words were "He knows we're going to get married but we just need a few years apart to fuck other people". Well if that isn't the best romantic line you've ever heard I don't know what is! So here I was once again single, left in debt and once again thinking what the hell is happening to my life. How had this happened to me again?

I'll cover more later on about my awakening and what happened next. He couldn't stand to see me standing on my own two feet, sabotaging me at every chance he could get. I had bailiffs knocking at my door as he refused to pay his car insurance and left it all registered to the flat. I was ill, defeated and worn out but he didn't stop there. Once I found out about this other woman four months on everything just made sense. He denied everything of course but what he didn't know was she admitted everything to me in a Facebook message. The fact they moved into his parents together, the same day we broke up, sums all of this up for me. So with his new woman you'd think that would be the end of all of this right? Wrong!

I had a close male friend at the time who did help me through a lot. Little did I know my best friend at the time had teamed up with my ex to 'bring me down' and was feeding back to him everything I was saying. My male friend got a series of threats from my ex saying he was welcome to the trash (me) and that I was scum. There was nothing going on and luckily my friends understood and could see what was really going on. He was certainly clever my ex, he worked around my entire friend group at the time manipulating and luring them into his trap just like he had done with me. Eventually all of my friends teamed up and turned against me to prove how horrible I was and what a nasty person I was. I felt like my world was over once again. I had worked so hard just even to survive, and now the people I thought I knew were trying to sabotage me. No matter what was said about me online I ignored it. I could have called the Police, I could have done a lot but I was better than that. By that point they couldn't touch me. The stronger I got the worse they all became. Slander, libel, harassment, the list goes on of the offences they all committed against myself and my business.

I remember the first day I went on ITV's 'This Morning' I felt so excited and happy. I hadn't heard from them all in months. I didn't announce I was on the show until ten minutes before to avoid any more sabotaging. The slot went incredibly well. Everybody was so supportive and impressed with how natural I was on live TV. A day later I was back home and sat with Selina & Chris, my friends. I went on my laptop to check my websites and my heart dropped. The message 'This website is unavailable because I'm a stuck up bitch' appeared across all of my websites. I instantly called my web guy who got it all taken down within minutes. Joe is certainly an angel in my life and he doesn't even know it. My ex was my old web guy and totally fucked everything up when we split up to hurt me. Joe had a tough time taking everything over, fixing my websites and gaining access to everything. He never asked any questions about why my ex would do this, he knew most of it anyway and just got on with it. Joe had tracked my ex's IP address down within seconds and we had a location and the time all of this happened. It happened while I was on air the day before so thousands upon thousands of people had seen that message by now and no one had alerted us. I was humiliated. This is my brand, my living, my everything and these people just wouldn't stop. It had been seven months now since we split, why wouldn't he just leave me alone. That evening I called the Police and I told them everything. I didn't care about the repercussions anymore. He wasn't going to stop until I took action. The Police were fantastic. Honestly, I can't thank Dorset Police enough for how efficiently they dealt with things and how quickly they acted. Within 24 hours he was arrested, charged and given an instant restraining order meaning he can never contact or come near me again. In this moment I felt so protected and safe for the first time in years, he couldn't get away with this anymore. The Police explained to me what would happen when it goes to court, the press it would attract because of what I do for a living and that he would potentially be sent to jail. They asked me whether I wanted to press charges and I froze, I couldn't be held responsible for ruining someone's life.

He had certainly ruined mine and continued to sabotage me, but I just couldn't do it. I wasn't the type of person who could do that to someone. So I dropped all the charges and he walked away a free man with this just noted on his record. I did this not only for myself, my businesses and my family but because one day I hope he'll change. I hope he'll treat her with respect and love, something he never did with me. I hope if he has children, he teaches them how to respect women and to act with love. I hope he himself awakens and realises that he can be more than this. It took me a long while to forgive all of this and move on. I haven't heard from him or any of my ex-friends he manipulated and turned against me for nearly two years now and I hope it stays that way.

All of this behaviour baffles us all still to this day. Why would he do all of this when he wanted to be with her? He got what he wanted so why continue to do what he did? Maybe it was jealousy, who knows. I knew deep down he had picked me because he knew he could never have me long term. He didn't pick me because I was weak or an easy target. He picked me because he saw exactly who I'd become, my strength, my power and the purity within myself. Something he would never have. Selina watched me go through all of this. She really has been an angel to me. Always picking me up, always helping me to believe amazing things were on the way. Holding me when I cried and helping me realise my worth, slowly but surely.

I always say that flat changed my life and it sure did. That flat became my sanctuary once he left and a safe place I could call my own. It never really felt like he had lived there and I completely made it my own style afterwards. Now I'm in my own home, it's weird, it feels like I never lived there at all. I don't miss it and I'm glad to have a brand new house with no previous memories or energy. It's completely mine. All of this had to happen for a reason. He awakened me, cleared out my entire life and broke me down until I was nothing. I rose from the ashes and created the life I had always dreamed of on my terms, no one else's, for the first time in my life. So thank you. I now know what role you played and you delivered me to my incredible future.

Awakening Queen

Now I was free and away from all negative influences, I
was able to listen to myself, to my needs and to what I truly
wanted more than anything. As the days past I felt stronger
and stronger, his influence was wearing off finally. I had to
hit rock bottom to start again. Many fear rock bottom, but
from losing everything and being at the point of wanting
to end my life, I can honestly say rock bottom was the best
fucking point to hit. I was a blank canvas, an empty vessel
ready to become the person I was destined to be. Rock
bottom became the most stable thing I had, it felt strong,
it felt like a roar from deep within me. Out of nowhere
I fucking became invincible. No one could ever hurt me
again because I'd hit my pain barrier. No one could detract
anything away from me ever again because I had nothing to
lose. This was finally my life, my rules, my terms and hell I
was about to flip everything in my life upside down and make
it fucking fabulous. Rachel my psychic was right. By the end
of this I did have the strength of a lion, a roar so strong no
one would dare bring her down again and a heart so big she
could love many.

I remember looking online for answers, for guidance and boy
did the Universe bring it. I typed into Google 'how to find a
positive in a negative situation' as I really didn't know what
I was looking for and a YouTube video came up by a lady
called Louise Hay. Louise's videos spoke to me in volume.
She never used the words 'Law of Attraction' but everything
she was saying sounded loving and made me feel like I was
on the right track. When I first heard the words Law of
Attraction, I thought it was a romantic thing and that I could

attract a man using it (well I did but not the point!). I don't remember how I found the words Law of Attraction. It must have been on some Google searches after Louise's videos. I then posted a status on Facebook asking if anyone could recommend Law of Attraction books and Selina replied. At this point Selina and I had recently reconnected. She had just told me she was pregnant despite the fact that we had never previously discussed anything spiritually or gone into that much depth. Selina recommended reading the book 'The Secret' by Rhonda Bryne. As my normal impatient self, I couldn't possibly wait for Amazon Prime's next day delivery and found the film version on Netflix.

On one of the many days I spent alone in the flat, I got some ironing and put 'The Secret' on Netflix. It was safe to say after the film had finished none of the ironing had been done. I was gripped, hooked to this crazy concept I'd just heard. The power to bring anything I can see in my mind's eye into my hands. Yes please! I became so obsessed with the topic ordering books, watching countless YouTube videos. The Law of Attraction became my new best friend and I studied it for hours upon hours, days upon days until shit started manifesting. Within the first month I manifested quite a few things. I started off small and these things came easily to me. For the first time in my life I was getting what I wanted. The Universe was finally responding to me. I remember how easily I manifested £500 for a pair of Christian Louboutin heels which I still to this day haven't bought. I then jokingly said 'Later on I'll manifest being debt free'. I actually forgot to do my money manifestation later that day and didn't even work out how much I needed to be debt free. Still, within five days I manifested £10,000, the exact amount to make me completely debt free, through new money within my business. So it really does prove how powerful our words really can be and how easily the Universe can bring things into fruition.

My friends at the time and my parents couldn't believe how I had literally turned my life around in a few weeks, from suicidal to loving herself and being debt free after three long years. I couldn't believe myself how easily the Universe made my dreams into reality. So I set big goals, the dream house, the husband, the career, the book deal, money, the lot. As I always say go hard or go home! I could feel something inside me awakening, a lion almost claiming her roar. I had momentum, drive and passion towards creating a life on my terms and boy did I get it. By giving the Universe clear instructions on what I would and wouldn't tolerate anymore, it opened up a clear path for abundance to start pouring in.

I worked on every part of my life, I mean everything. My health, my fitness, my mental health, my self-love, my anger and all my flaws. I wanted to almost construct the Emma I knew I was meant to be all along. I started saying yes to myself and no to others. It felt selfish at the time but it is so important that we take time out for ourselves and nurture ourselves so we can give to others. Many people find it weird that I absolutely love my own company, for months it haunted me being alone in that flat with no one beside me. After realising how powerful my own company is and how I can reflect, meditate and realign so easily. Now, whenever anything troubles me or threatens my happiness I simply set a date with myself and go within. I am a giver, a healer and will certainly help anyone and everyone. That's my job, but I can't help anyone if I can't help myself first.

To realign I love nothing more than a pink Himalayan salt bath or an Epsom salt bath. Both are really easy to get your hands on and both will make you a bath addict. I can't explain to you what these salts do because it is simply magic. I always feel connected, realigned and focused after simply bathing in these and meditating. Another way I like to realign if I'm feeling a bit off is to sit and work on my gratitude, so I am really sending love to everyone in every situation and questioning how can I allow myself to feel even more gratitude in the present moment?

When I started the Law of Attraction I was left in a very tight financial situation. My ex had left me with our flat and rent to pay for another seven months. That was £5,950 I wasn't expecting to have to pay by myself but somehow I did it. I managed to manifest, doubling, even tripling my income to cover my bills and to live comfortably. I couldn't believe it myself that by removing him from my life how much abundance and happiness awaited me. Life became more enjoyable at this point and I could see a future for myself, my business and with the man of my dreams.

I honestly don't know what got me through these days. It was hard to install all this faith in the hope I would still have a roof over my head, food on the table and hot water. I had no choice, I had nothing to lose and everything to gain! Even now two years on it shocks me just how much everything has come into fruition and how quickly. Even some manifestations that have taken a year, really in the grand scheme of things it's no time at all. In my most recent reading with Rachel she said that I won't be moving home for another year and that I will in fact buy this next house with Mr Right. In that moment I felt disappointed. Crazy I know, seeing as in that moment I should of been like "Omg this is amazing, my credit score must get magically fixed, I must manifest enough money for a deposit and I get to live with Mr Right". In fact I felt disappointed it wasn't happening sooner, a whole twelve months away! Now this reaction makes me laugh. Think how much changes in a year, and let's not forget divine timing. The Universe knows when it's bringing this house and money into my life, it won't be rushed and it certainly won't bring it closer even if I sulk hard enough. What I should have thought is, great I have another year to save up, clear my credit file, work on my businesses and other important projects, travel the world, see my friends, enjoy my own space and alone time. Let's face it, I will soon miss living alone once it's gone! So now I'm looking at the positives and how quickly a year has flown by. It's no time at all. We often block ourselves and our manifestations by falling under the illusion of time. The Universe doesn't listen to time it listens to your vibration, so if you're always seeing something in your future guess where it's staying? You need to see these manifestations in the now, it's happening now. You deserve it all and remember to be grateful for what the Universe is blessing you with right now.

After a few months of studying the Law of Attraction, I
knew I wanted more. I needed more sparkle, more energy
and to dip my feet more into the pool of the Universe. I
started looking into Angels. I've always been guided by what
I'd call Angels and always felt someone was watching over
me. The first book I read was by the lovely Kyle Gray *'Raise
Your Vibration'*. I adore Kyle's work now, but this book once
again blew my world up. It opened me up to the realm of
Angels and how we can call upon these magnificent beings to
help us along our journey and calling in life. I called upon my
Angel army to heal, protect and to guide me to my future and
boy did they. I did the entire 111 day practices in Kyle's book
and felt amazing, I was certainly in the vortex! Although I'd
done all the work, found countless white feathers and signs
they were present, I still don't think I believed my Angels
were helping me. It was only when I had a reading with
Rachel that she said "Wow you are surrounded by an army
of Angels all protecting you and guiding you. They want
you to know they've been listening", that I realised…wow
this shit works. I always feel comforted knowing that Angels
surround me and it's not as scary as I once thought it might
be. I don't hear them or see them but little signs show me
they are close and being one badass army up there shining
their light down on me.

I then discovered any incredible man on YouTube called
Brad Yates. I've got a lot of love for this man and he has
given me a lot of love for both myself and my life which
I never thought possible. EFT or Emotional Freedom
Technique is certainly a weird looking one, when you first

do it you do think 'If someone could see me right now, I know they'd think I've lost it'. Appearance aside, EFT is probably one of the best techniques I've learnt along the way to instantly get me out of any mood, sadness or anger. You name it, you can snap out of it in under ten minutes using this technique. The first video I ever watched of Brad's was about self-love. I remember feeling a surge of emotion come over me so strong I burst out crying for at least ten minutes. It felt like a wave of relief, the emotions I'd been bottling up for so long had been finally released and the past emotional trauma healed. You do need to keep up with these practices, there are so many you can do for different emotions whether it's to heal, to attract money, to getting in the vortex, Brad has you covered.

EFT is often referred to as "psychological acupressure", the technique works by releasing blockages within the energy system which are the source of emotional intensity and discomfort. These blockages in our energy system, in addition to challenging us emotionally, often lead to limiting beliefs and behaviours and an inability to live life harmoniously. An EFT treatment involves the use of your fingers rather than needles to tap on the end points of energy meridians that are situated just beneath the surface of the skin. I actually didn't realise how widely known EFT is within the medical profession. It seems so spiritual but it bloomin' works. Now whenever I need to lift my moods or release a negative emotion, I turn to EFT. I'm heading to one of Brad's events here in the UK in December. I'm really excited as I feel the energy of the room will be incredible!

EFT for me has not only given me a gateway to instant release and healing, it has given me release in all aspects of my life. I first used it to heal my heart after my breakup, to build up my confidence and to teach me how to love and accept myself finally. Simply it helped heal every aspect of my broken soul. I then used it to help manifest my desires, to help maintain my high vibration and to keep me in the vortex of good feelings. Now I do all of the above still but I choose one of Brad's videos I most feel drawn to it at that time. Whether it's becoming a money magnet or to simply build up more self-love, these EFT practices are so vital in any Spiritual Queen's life.

By this point, I was well on my way to leading a rich spiritual life under my new guidance from the Universe. I then started to discover my idol Tony Robbins and his incredible videos. Although Tony never directly refers to the Law of Attraction in his work, he certainly does it and preaches it! I loved how Tony constructed the perfect life he now lives and this is the inspirational story I needed to hear to realise that I too could help transform millions of people's lives. I love Tony's connection with God and how he always said to himself 'I'm surrounded by God's wealth' each day before he became the Tony you see today. My story is very similar in the fact that I have almost designed my entire life with the help of divine timing and intuition. I hated my old life so much that now I don't settle for any less than magnificent.

My friends and family always refer to me as the female Tony Robbins. While that is the ultimate compliment for me, I don't want to be a copy or unauthentic in my work.

We are all different and we all bring a different message into this world, so for me I'm Emma Mumford and she has an incredible message to deliver just as Tony Robbins does. Eventually, I'd love to hold my own seminars across the world, inspiring people and getting everyone to start believing in their own unlimited potential. Just to add, yes I totally will get you all jumping up and down to motivational beats because it feels bloody amazing when you raise everyone's vibration in one room. Tony really taught me how to aim big and that if he could do it so could I. He helped me a lot to realise that I couldn't heal my ex and that really I did need to move on and raise my standards. All of this information I got from his Youtube videos and books. Meeting him of course was the best day of my life (so far), Tony if you're reading this THANK YOU. You helped me to see my sparkle, my worth and that my past doesn't define me.

Although Tony's work is mainly based around business, which is great because it's helped me to grow my businesses and see my next steps as a girl boss over the coming years, one thing I've always been good at in my Extreme Couponing business is getting the money I know I'm worth. For instance paid advertisement has never been a struggle for me because I know my brand's worth and what I will and won't accept. This mentality also came from Tony's work. The one thing I'm not good at is in my Emma Mumford business, which is essentially my life coaching, author work, YouTube and Blogging, I never used to get the money I know I should have been receiving.

Friends of mine sometimes charge double what I do for a blog post and they have a tenth of my following online. It's odd but I'm constantly working on and working towards that belief of worthiness in my new business. I always feel like well why is my work better than anyone else and how could I get away with charging that? Simple, raise your standards and believe in your awesomeness. The Universe will always meet you there and be supporting you.

That limiting belief is exactly what I thought when I first started my Extreme Couponing business and started charging for advertising. Yet, somehow I overcame it and believed in my brand enough to start manifesting more and more opportunities. I think it's easier to see a brand's worth more than your own personal worth, but at the end of the day it all comes down to self-love. When I set the bar high with the Universe on what I would and wouldn't accept into my life, I upped my game entirely and I raised my prices. At first it put a few people off and I did think 'What have I done!'. Shortly after this problem was solved because I was manifesting better quality clients who actually respected my brand. I enjoyed my work once again, I grew a new passion for my work, it was finally fulfilling me because I was aligned and making more money than I'd ever had in my life. Whether you run your own business or you're employed, it's important to remember that at any time we can raise our standards, raise our game and create the life of our dreams. I hope by this point in my book you're starting to realise that 'Damn, we really can create our realities!'

After delving even more into spirituality I then discovered my love for crystals. When I was younger I remember I bought some crystals from a spiritual shop in Boscastle in Cornwall. I was about thirteen at the time and had no idea what I was doing. The crystals felt weird and I didn't like them much. We returned home to find so many electrical faults had happened in the house. Instantly my parents blamed these new crystals I'd obtained and before I knew it they'd been disposed of. As this was my first experience with crystals, it took me a long time to trust the countless people telling me to get some. I didn't see a benefit and I thought what's the point?! The first crystal I purchased was when I was having nightmares every single night about my ex very early on in my awakening. I hadn't slept for weeks and the haunting nightmares were becoming too disruptive. I knew at this point I had to open up and allow the wonderful energy of crystals to heal and awaken me. I did some research online and learnt how to cleanse them, ask for their help and which ones would help with sleeping and healing. So off I went to my local crystal shop and bought myself a Rose Quartz and Amethyst crystal. I've never looked back since, and it's safe to say my crystal collection has grown into an obsession which I'm certainly proud of. After buying those two crystals, I have slept every single night undisturbed. I used to put the Rose Quartz in my bra during the day to attract love wherever I went and that certainly helped both heal my heart and to show me real love does exist.

Cleansing crystals is really simple, you can wave incense over them, pour filtered water on them or cleanse them in the sea. For me personally, I love running them under filtered water and that's what clears my crystals. It will be different for everyone. Once cleared, which is really important to do after buying crystals or when they don't feel right anymore, you can then hold them in your hand and set your intentions. So for example with the Amethyst crystal my intentions were to sleep easier, remove negative dreams, to heal myself and to protect myself. Each crystal has a different meaning and you can find these out online or your local crystal shop will be able to help you out. I always love putting my crystals out on a full moon and new moon to recharge and absorb some glorious moon energy. This is also a way to cleanse crystals under the moon, and crystals do love a good moon bathe!

You can use crystals for all aspects of your life. For me, they protect, heal and guide me spiritually. I've also given some to my dear friend Annie who was battling breast cancer last year and who is now successfully in remission. Annie was so cautious when I gave these to her as she was a complete skeptic. I gave her both a Rose Quartz and Amethyst to help heal her, protect her and to help her feel supported and loved during her treatment. A few months later when I next saw her, the first thing she said was how amazing these crystals were. She too had problems sleeping due to chemotherapy, but since having this Amethyst crystal by her bedside each night, she slept like a baby. I'd love to think these crystals helped heal her during this time and gave her comfort she so deserved. It's incredible that she is now in remission and swears by crystals, which is great to see!

Crystals are simply amazing and so many people will agree with me on this one. Do keep them out of reach from other people, as you will find that if other people touch your crystals, they'll suck all the lovely energy out that you've created. They're very sensitive to energy, so if you do create a little shrine then keep it by your bedside or up high! Not only are they beautiful and great home decor pieces, they can help to emit positivity around your home and out and about. Quite a few people I know have a crystal keyring on their car keys or wear crystal jewellery so that they can carry these precious crystals around with them all day and be protected.

As I kept awakening more and more, I wanted to eat healthier and nurture my body. I decided to walk more, start running and even took up Yoga. Yoga has to be my favourite practice to keep fit. Surprisingly it helped me lose three dress sizes and puts me in such a fantastic mind frame afterwards. I normally watch '*Yoga with Adriene*' on YouTube. She is simply awesome and I connect with her videos the most. My body became more and more sensitive to bad food and I have even now developed a dairy intolerance. I've become allergic to caffeine and have given up alcohol. All of this was natural though. My allergies have naturally worsened over the last year and caffeine made me feel awful, it has the complete opposite effect, I fall asleep! Giving up alcohol is quite a new venture for me. I never thought I would want to but once again it happened so naturally I didn't even notice. I always felt so dulled down after a night out with the girls and found it hard to raise my vibration the next day. I have now been six months without drinking alcohol and honestly it was the best unintentional decision I've ever made. I feel so much more awakened and in touch with my intuition. My diet has changed considerably. Yes, I do still love pizza more than life, but I am conscious that I'm making better food decisions and watching what I put into my lovely body. I've cut out all aspartame products as this chemical is awful for you and can cause dementia. I've switched my salt to pink himalayan salt (the most purest salt) and even switched to some Vegan products to help with my dairy intolerance.

I didn't decide any of this, the Universe had its own plans. A year and a half on I feel so much more awakened, healthy, I love my body and I know I'm looking after myself. Now ask yourself the same question 'What am I putting in my body?' it will certainly scare you when you look into what is actually put into our food.

Finally, another practice I've embraced is Moon Cycles. I first heard about this on YouTube and followed different astrology horoscopes, then I came across new moon & full moon practices which really got my spiritual juices flowing. I embraced once again another practice I would have laughed at before and started worshiping the moon. I put all my crystals out both on a new moon and full moon to 'moon bathe' as I like to call it, your beauties will absorb amazing moon energy and it will really energise them to help aid you. I've also incorporated moon cycles to help manifest money which I will cover in full later on. The new moon is incredibly powerful and can really add incredible energy to your manifestations. I make lists on the new moon of what I'd like to manifest in the coming month and every single month I tick every goal off! It's also really important to write at the beginning of your new moon list 'I manifest these things into my life now or something better for my highest good'.

I don't tend to do that many full moon practices but when I do they are equally as powerful. The full moon is all about letting go and releasing old beliefs and energy. I simply set up a little alter with candles and my favourite crystals, write a list of everything I want to let go of, even if it's really negative. I then burn this list in a bowl and they say the quicker it burns the more you're ready to let go of the problem. I have looked slightly crazy doing these practices before. I remember my best friend Selina and I did this when I lived in a top floor flat. We had the window wide open in the kitchen to prevent the fire alarms going off and it was right in the middle of a thunder storm. To any passersby or neighbours we must have looked crazy burning things out of my kitchen window. Anyway it bloody works even if we did look a little silly! Now luckily I have a beautiful garden so I would strongly advise for health and safety reasons, doing this practice outside, thunder storm is optional but adds a desired dramatic effect.

"Rock bottom became the
solid foundation on which
I rebuilt my life."

—J.K.Rowling

Universal Queen

I've never shared publicly my meditation stories up until this point. I always felt that I would be judged or people would see it as too freakin' weird. Yeah I still get that, the fear of being judged. I get that I'm different we all are, not everyone has seen their daughter ten years before she will be born, it's not exactly a topic for the dinner table. The only person who I've told everything to is my best friend Selina as she's actually quite a big part of it. So let me take you back to when I was sixteen, the little ugly duckling Emma as I like to call her. School was really hard for me. I remember opening up my GCSE results and just thinking what the hell am I going to do with five GCSEs. That summer I remember being at an all time low, I was very isolated where I lived and I couldn't go out very often and see my friends. I remember using all my pocket money to buy a Buddhism book from Waterstones and declared myself Buddhist as God just wasn't working out for me at that time. Where was he when I needed him?

My peers laughed at me when I told them about this amazing book I'd purchased and how I was learning about all these great ways to meditate. I'm not convinced I read this in the book, but really I must have read this process somewhere. It was to imagine a happy place, a place you can go to and call your own. My happy place is in a meadow. It's a warm summer's evening and the wind is always gently blowing through the fields as I arrive. There is a beautiful stream running through the field with a massive oak tree by the river side. There is also a bridge connecting the field to the castle, which symbolised my future. Of course being a Cinderella fangirl I had to have a castle! All of this came so naturally and still eight years on I see this scene as vividly as I did the first time.

I used to go there every single day and just sit and wish that my life would get better, that people would understand me and that I could understand myself. I must have done this for three months over the summer holidays and I genuinely think if I had kept it up I would have awoken a lot earlier in my life. One day while being in my happy place, a small brunette girl appeared. At first I was like get out of my happy place...but this little girl was not leaving! She started to call me Mummy, yeah really weird...and then continued to tell me that if I wrote my heart's desires on the leaves of the oak tree and send them down the river they would come true. So with nothing to lose I followed this girl's instructions and I know exactly what I wrote down eight years ago, and can say I have 100% of what I asked for back then. Law of Attraction much! One of the things I remember asking for was to be self-employed and to be well known for what I did. In that moment I knew my success would be online and that what I was going to do hadn't been created yet. After seeing this girl numerous times in my happy place, a second girl turned up eventually, this time a blonde haired, blue eyed girl who was younger than the first. She too called me Mummy but it never felt right, she didn't look like me and her name was Ella. It must have been about two years later when I went for my first ever psychic reading that I finally asked who on earth are these girls?

The psychic replied "Yes the first girl is your daughter. She's extremely spiritual and has been sent to guide you through this time of your life". The second she had no idea as I was meant to have a boy after my first daughter. Confused as to who Ella was, I simply thought this all must be a figment of my imagination right? Wrong! For many years I went to this place, saw these girls and one time they showed me who I would marry. I only saw him from the back but he had dark hair, slim build and pretty much looked like my Mr Right. Maybe I manifested it, maybe I saw a glimpse of him, who knows! I still find all of this absolutely crazy that my daughter has been in my life, years before she has even been thought about and yes I do know her name! The first time I heard it I thought why on earth would I pick that, but equally it felt perfect. It was never my choice and for the last eight years my friends and even my family have called her by her name, it's surreal but I can't wait to meet her.

By the age of eighteen I had changed dramatically and had given up on my Buddhist adventure. I had started working at a coffee chain and became very human, very quickly. I dulled down and worked extremely hard to get money and prove to myself that I was worthy of a good job. After meeting my first boyfriend I would say I was completely atheist. I had no belief in anything anymore; my daughter, my happy place was a distant memory. Had it all been a figment of my imagination to get me through a tough time in my life? I spoke about this earlier but by the end of the first relationship I was Christian once again, God had sent my 'saviour' and I was 'free' at last. Once I'd moved back to my parents' house I felt my spirituality trying to creep back in. I would meditate but not much would happen, my daughter would be there, but it felt dark, it felt tainted, something wasn't right.

I first discovered Rachel Rendell on Facebook back in 2014. Rachel has become such a big part of my life now and has guided me through the last five years. I don't know what made me go to a psychic, I guess I wanted answers, I wanted spoilers, I wanted confirmation that I'd get my happily ever after I'd promised myself all those years ago. I thought I finally had my prince charming so a psychic would confirm this for me right? Well my first reading with Rachel certainly did not confirm my second ex was my husband at all. It was a positive reading and I got to hear from my gorgeous nan who I miss so dearly. I remember feeling such love and happiness from hearing her and knowing that the only way was up after a few turbulent years. I heard great things about my business, that I'd be on TV (This Morning) and all about the white flat I'd move into with my ex. All of what Rachel said came true including the flat, shame she wasn't told about all the bullshit and hurt after moving into that flat! A pre-warning would have been great, but really it was meant to cut me open to heal and awaken me. Over the next few years I did my meditation practices a few times a year, it just didn't have the same effect as it used to. Rachel never mentioned any children to me so once again I just believed I had imagined the whole thing. Maybe it was just wishful thinking?

Let's skip to April 2016, the week leading up to the split with my second ex-boyfriend. I was low, lower and more depressed than I'd ever been in my entire life. I wanted the world to just end it all. I spoke to God every single day, begging for help, begging for him to just end all this pain and suffering. I had lost every ounce of who I was, I was empty, weak and ready to leave this cruel world behind. Then something spoke to me louder than ever before, my daughter saying meditate, meditate now! I was in the bath, and my ex was in the living room playing on his game console as per usual. It felt weird going to this happy place when all I could do was see darkness. It was easy though. I remember how good it felt to be there once again. The cool wind blowing through my hair, walking through the long grassy field, up to the tree to make my wishes. My daughter was there once again but no Ella, I asked where she was and she simply replied "she's moved on". This was weird seeing as I was meant to be Ella's Mum also? I remember looking into my daughter's hazel eyes and thinking this is too real, all of this feels real, her touch, her words, why on earth am I seeing all of this when my reality is too painful to bare. She led me up to the bridge and made me cross over to the castle, one thing I had never been able to do before, she was delivering me to my future. I remember entering the castle and walking upstairs to a small room overlooking the field. I remember a man entering the room and he stood behind me. I believe this was my spirit guide/guardian angel, this wasn't my husband, but he handed me a newborn baby boy and said this is your reward for going through the next year of your life. What on earth was going on here? I remember opening my eyes back in the flat and thinking one day Emma your crazy imagination will serve you well. I honestly thought I was nuts at this point.

After the split I immediately called Rachel my psychic and booked in with her, I needed to know whether my ex was coming back and why on earth the 'love of my life' had left me. I needed answers once again. What Rachel said changed my life forever, he wasn't coming back, he was never meant for me. My nan was very angry at him (I had no idea why until I found about the cheating four months later). Rachel told me someone else was on the way and that I would be happy again. She also told me how my son had just chosen me to be his mother and that I would be a god mother very soon. I love that our children choose us, I've heard this from a few people now. I couldn't believe it, I had seen my son just days before in my happy place. For the first time in my life I didn't feel crazy, I felt like everything had started to align. I had two other readings with two separate psychics as a check that Rachel just wasn't giving me the answers I needed to hear. I just couldn't accept what she had said about my ex being a karmic soulmate, it explained the connection for sure, but nothing made any sense. The male psychic I went to detailed everything completely wrong, he said my ex would come back to me, yeah I'm certainly glad that never happened! The one thing he did get right was that I have the potential for a third child. One girl and two boys, well that thought didn't excite me much I'll be honest! Childbirth has never really appealed to me, so the thought of having a third freaked me out more than it excited me! The other lady psychic I went to again got everything wrong and said I would have this son in 2017. Well I can tell you now that definitely has not happened! Rachel has still to this day been the only psychic who has told me so much and been 100% accurate on absolutely everything.

Rachel didn't give me much information on my future or Mr Right until January 2017. In the two readings I had after the split it was mainly regarding my ex and all the bullshit I had to go through to get my happily ever after. Once again every single thing Rachel said came true, even predicting the test man that would come into my life before meeting Mr Right. She said he would live in London and he did. This is famously the 70% perfect man, to be honest I think the topless pictures on his Instagram was what was swaying me to thinking this was my dream man. I'm still convinced this guy is secretly gay. Looking back I know this guy was an important part in the grand plan, without him being an utter arsehole I never would have met the people who would have told me all about my Mr Right and I never would have met the other Rachel who gave me a past life regression reading. So really I do want to thank this guy and his abs for being a twat because you led me straight down the right spiritual path!

After my reading in January Rachel confirmed to me 2017 was the year I'd meet Mr Right, that I would get married and keep my surname. She confirmed my children for the first time, their names and that I'd be buying a three bed house within the next three years. I was fully awakened by this time, but I can't tell you the relief I felt when Rachel confirmed everything I had been seeing in my happy place for all these years.

Since the time I meditated in the bath and saw my son for the first time, I haven't been able to get to my happy place, every time I do no one is there anymore and it feels different now but still in a really positive way. Maybe my daughter did deliver me to my future, she certainly did look after me and guide me for the last seven years. Her name means Rainbow and I never knew it until I looked it up a few weeks ago. I love this meaning because she really has been my rainbow throughout all the storms. Without the rain, there would be no rainbow.

The next message from the Universe was from my Angel squad, well I like to think I have my own Angel squad up there keeping my spiritual arse in line. After reading Kyle Gray's *'Raise Your Vibration'* I felt super empowered and awakened. I had summoned my angels to help heal me after my split and they were guiding me through everyday life. I love using Angel cards for advice and little spoilers, it always feels so loving and they are extremely accurate. I remember being in my flat and walking into the bathroom, all the windows were shut, but as I entered the room I heard someone call my name as clear as day in my right ear. Shocked I turned around to see no one. I checked my phone in case I pocket dialled someone. There is still no explanation for what I heard, but it felt loving and like a reminder that they're there helping me. Rachel also said in one of her later readings that I have a whole army of angels looking after me, it feels amazing to hear this and I certainly have had a few guardian angel experiences in my life.

The next person to enter my life was Momoko, a sweet numerology lady. I first found out about her from the guy I was seeing in London. It was exciting to have a numerology reading and find out about why numbers stalked me so much. This reading was certainly life changing. Six is my life number, same as my Mr Right's and thirty-three is my destiny number. I have used the number three, six, three throughout my entire life; all the numbers described me so well. Momoko also said that this year would be a great year to write a book (well here I am!). She also said I'd meet Mr Right this year and that I'm currently in year three of my nine year cycle. I'd heard about these cycles before and how every nine years we all start a new life cycle. I remember even the pre-meditation Momoko put me in felt amazing and so full of positive, bright energy. That's what spurred me on to get my thirty-three tattoo on my wrist because everything just suddenly made sense.

A few months later Momoko told me about her friend over in America who had just started doing soulmate readings. Well hello! I immediately got in touch with him and booked in for the next day. He picked up on my Mr Right's energy straight away, he explained a confident extremely spiritual man who would be everything I'd ever asked for. I won't lie, the person he described scared me because of how confident he sounded. I did think, why on earth would the Universe send me someone so cocky?!

The psychic was very descriptive in his reading so I had a lot to go on, he told me that I'd need to be more adventurous and spontaneous in order to attract him and that it would be within the next seven months. So when Mr Right did come into my life I had a massive shock just as he had said I would because Mr Spiritually Cocky was actually Mr completely the opposite!

The psychic did describe his soul name as Leonardo which when I heard Mr Right say this name time and time again I was like shit this has to be real! Leonardo is a massive part of his life and I remember telling Selina the same night and she started freaking out exactly like I had, we'd found him! I was confused about why Mr Right didn't walk in as this man the psychic had described but I knew I had to let it go and allow the Universe to deliver whatever was for my highest good. The more I get to know him the more I do see it now. I think when you first get to know someone you never really see their true personality until further along the line. Hell I was holding back the weirdness trust me! I mean after being single for a year I was extremely worried about how I'd tell this guy, by the way I knew you were coming. I manifested you and yeah you're my twin flame. Luckily, he felt the same way. It's hard when you know someone can awaken to just hold back and not overload them with a million Law of Attraction books, I have learnt to be patient. Even if it never happens, he supports me, listens to my spiritual talk and takes an interest, that's all I'd ask for anyway. After my reading, I felt so much love for this dream man already who I'd never even met and this certainly helped me recognise it was Mr Right when he arrived. I find it simply amazing just how much universal intelligence we really can tap into and learn about before our time. I seriously am the most impatient person though. I dread to think how much money I've spent on all of these readings over the last year, but do you know what, I don't regret it. I've met some amazing people with incredible talents and learnt so much about myself and my future so it's been worth every single penny.

More than anything it's taught me to trust myself here, I didn't need these readings. Yes, they were great but I could trust the Universe and trust myself no matter what.

Since writing the above I've had a past life regression reading with a lovely welsh lady called Rachel. Momoko introduced me to her and after reading Rebecca Campbell's *"Light Is The New Black"* book, I knew I wanted to delve into my past lives and see what I could uncover. I wasn't too sure what to expect with this reading as Rachel did say I'd get messages and shown things throughout. The meditation Rachel put me in was really relaxing and I was fully aware at all times, once I'd entered my Akashic library through meditation it was an odd feeling almost like I'd been here before. Rachel asked me to imagine a white light beaming out the top of my head into the sky, I froze. I had been doing this every single time I meditated to get to my happy place. For all those years I wasn't meditating, I was actually connecting to the Universe and asking for messages! It's no wonder my daughter and everything else came through to me all those times with messages. For around forty minutes I was in this deep meditation receiving all sorts of wonderful and loving messages from my daughter (of course!), my nan and even Mr Right's energy. This was the first time I allowed any messages to come through to me and my daughter sure had a lot to say (she definitely takes after me). It was odd. Here I could see her really vividly, her beautiful long brown hair, her hazel eyes and how much she looks like Mr Right. She certainly has my attitude though and I could tell she had a lot to tell me!

A lot of random images, names and words were shown to me but a lot of it didn't really make sense to me. My Nan came forward with another woman who felt like she was on Mr Right's side, saying how happy they were for us and that at our wedding there will be two white doves and they'll be holding them symbolising they are with us which felt amazing to hear and see this. My daughter then took me to my happy place. I couldn't believe it, I was able to get there again after so long. It felt so different this time round, everything was vibrant, the long grass felt brighter, softer and more vivid. It was like someone had turned up the colour and vividness of the whole place. Mr Right was there and our son, we all just sat in the grass of the field watching the sunset and it felt so right.

I can't describe the happiness I felt seeing my son's face for the first time so vividly and seeing how he'll look just like me as a baby with lighter brown hair and my button nose. I felt like she wanted me to see and feel this so I knew it was on the way and to not worry. I was then back in the library and she kept telling me there was something in my tummy, I laughed and said "Not yet, maybe in a few years!" She kept going on and on and laughing at how she was very soon going to be making an appearance and I remember saying "No you're not, don't be silly!" I then saw a visual of my womb with a baby growing in it. It was safe to say I was freaking the fuck out by this point! My spirit guide then appeared and said that it was all happening how it should be and that I shouldn't worry, they'll take care of all the obstacles I've created to stop her from happening. The last scene she showed me was on a glass balcony of an lovely house overlooking the sea. Mr Right and I were much older by this point and grey. We were stood slow dancing together while the sun set in the distance. I could see his face so clearly, smell him and see every wrinkle on his old self. It felt like we were celebrating our life together and still very much in love. So when Rachel pulled me out of this meditation it was safe to say I was in shock. I had never experienced anything like this before. It was all so real and so vivid like premonitions of what was to come.

Rachel then told me what she had seen and written down. She explained that my power animal was a lion (of course) and that my strength reflected this. I'm a seeker and warrior who's always looking for more. I'm small but mighty (not sure 6ft counts as small?), that I'm an old soul, which I knew anyway. Rachel then proceeded to talk about my womb, to which I replied "I think I know what you're going to say!" She asked whether I wanted kids as my womb is preparing itself and is ready. Well excuse me womb, I was kind of planning you to be ready in a few years not after three months of meeting Mr Right! Rachel said that I needed to make a decision as to whether my daughter comes now and that I need to be extremely careful as she's on the way. Rachel also spoke about some past lives and my about my spirit guide who is guiding me to success. It's odd because all week I'd had signs from my daughter through white butterflies, flowers, rainbows, the whole lot. Selina's saw it also and we both felt she had something big to say. I also said to Selina that week something big is about to happen in our relationship I can feel it. So here I am royally freaking out at this news, my daughter's telling me it's happening, the Universe is saying it also, my friends all told me way before I met Mr Right they thought I'd get pregnant early on. I even had a sense things would move extremely fast but chose to ignore all of this and use the Law of Attraction to delay it all. It's funny I actually made a pact with Selina months before I met Mr Right that I wouldn't be intimate with him for twelve weeks, one to make sure he was the one and secondly as I'd been told I'd get pregnant early on by so many people and friends' intuitions that I didn't want it to happen. Well the twelve weeks certainly didn't happen, and now it looks like we could all be right. Rachel's reading, however freaky and shocked it's left me, was incredible. I don't think I'd do it again, but I did learn a lot about myself and why I put up so many guards. She gave me some great crystals to work with and told me which birds to look out for as my spirit guide was sending them to help me move forwards. I'm not really sure how to end this chapter now, I wasn't expecting my daughter to be saying that to me! Can I ground my unborn child yet for showing me all of this?

Finally, I hear you all asking so who was Ella? Well I asked myself the same question over the last two years. So in April 2016 she disappeared from my meditation space and my daughter told me she had 'moved on'. In April 2016 my best friend Selina became pregnant, in December Isabella was born and became my gorgeous goddaughter. It's odd as when Ella called me 'Mum' in my visions, it always felt off it didn't feel right and why did I have one brunette daughter with hazel eyes and one blonde with blue eyes? I forgot all about

Ella until one day I was telling Selina about this story and how weird it was she just disappeared. Well thanks to Selina for finally putting the puzzle pieces together and made the connection straight away...Ella was Isabella! Now Isabella is the age Ella was in my visions I see it so clearly. It's freaky but such a blessing at the same time as I had no idea Selina was pregnant until much later on in her pregnancy and no idea she would call her Isabella. It explains so much now and is such a beautiful connection to my beautiful goddaughter I will always cherish.

"Without the rain, there would be no rainbow."

—Gilbert K. Chesterton

Spiritual Queen

So now you know my full spiritual path. I always felt uneasy sharing this on my YouTube channel because of the fear of being judged or laughed at. It's silly I know, but with such vivid messages and intuition it's still something I feel that will be mocked. I want to talk more in depth about my religion here and how it's affected me over the years. As I've explained previously, I was raised a Christian and believed in God up until the age of sixteen.

My parents had me Christened and I went to a Church of England school, so really God has been a big part of my life growing up. I remember we always had to say grace before lunch time at school and even morning prayer was part of our daily assemblies. I then for a year explored Buddhism and spirituality loosely through various books. When I was twenty I became Christian once again after being an atheist for several years, before finally at the age of twenty-two I gave up on religion all together. No one ever forced me to believe in any of these religions, it was always my choice and what I felt guided to at the time. I think I turned my back on God so many times simply because I felt he'd abandoned me. I felt like he'd left me with all this pain and suffering when in reality I'd done this to myself.

Yes, it was part of my journey and I had to go through it but I remember being so angry with God that he hadn't just miraculously made my life better. I never felt listened to when praying, I always felt like I was missing out and that it was only for a select few. I can't tell you why I felt like this but maybe I brought it on myself by believing I wasn't being listened to. In my eyes now, religion doesn't exist. I of course respect anyone's beliefs and views to do with religion, and I do believe most religions are very similar. They all reflect love which is essentially what religion is and many mention Law of Attraction in one way or another throughout. I believe in God, the Universe or the Source, whatever you want to call it. I don't believe it's an old man sat on a white cloud up there looking down on us all and I don't believe that God is cruel or unkind.

What I do believe is that God is within us all, we are all part of the same energy and connected to the Source. We are all capable of manifesting incredible things into our lives and everyone is entitled to the same amount of abundance, wealth, success and love there is certainly enough to go around. I don't believe in heaven and hell, I believe there is a heaven like structure in which our souls go to once we've departed from this world. I also believe we choose our paths, our destiny, our parents and that life is not happening to us, it's happening for us.

Losing my religion was the best thing that ever happened to me, because now I actually incorporate a mixture of religions into my everyday life. I would class myself as spiritual for certain, but I don't limit myself to anything. Before I always felt restrained and chained to religions, now I follow my own beliefs and it feels right. It feels authentic to me. I do feel connected to God and certainly feel like he's listening to me now. When I first started my Law of Attraction journey I did still use the name God, now I prefer to call it the Universe. It's not because anything has changed within me, I just feel more connected to that name and feel that's the right option for me. There is no right or wrong answer though, I believe every person's journey and relationship with the Universe is unique to the individual, so always do whatever feels right for you.

It always angers me when people are so quick to blame religion on all the wars and conflict in today's society. Religion is not to blame here, the Governments and people in charge are. The media wants us to believe that religion, spirituality and any form of belief in God and more in life is frowned upon. There are extremists in all walks of life and religions. Most religions are very peaceful and practice love, we're all doing the same thing essentially, loving one another and being grateful for everything we have. Maybe it would be easier for people to speak about their beliefs if the media portrayed a much more positive spin on religions and beliefs. We are all human, we all have souls and we can choose to do good or bad in the world. No God would ever want harm, violence or blood to be shed in this Universe. So that leads me on to a question I get asked frequently. Why do bad things happen to good people?

Honestly, it's a tough one to answer, especially when someone has passed away. We all have a purpose here on this earth, a life path and journey we complete. Sadly some people's impact on the earth can be much shorter than others and the holes they leave in our hearts can be just as big. This is why it's important to be grateful for every person that's in your life, for each day you wake up and the chance to create more memories. Each day is a blessing and one motto I've started to live by is 'Who's life have I changed today?' I know

I'm here to be a healer so for me helping someone every single day of my life is extremely important and fulfilling. It's not about success for me, how many followers I can get or even the money. It's about the number of lives I can impact and show the light of the Universe. The Universe doesn't want anyone to suffer or to be in pain, sure losing someone is painful, I can't take that away, but celebrate their incredible life. Celebrate the impact they've made in the world. They completed their life mission and that's a great reason to rejoice.

After becoming Spiritual I did keep my views and beliefs quiet for quite some time. I always felt judged around my old friends and the fact white butterflies were stalking me didn't help matters. I knew what I was seeing and experiencing was real, psychics had validated it and the Universe had validated it. Explaining it to non-believers can be daunting and painful sometimes if they simply don't support you. When I began to mention the words manifesting, the Universe and positivity around my old friends and family I did get some weird looks. I genuinely think they thought I was mad by this point and had lost the plot. They couldn't believe that I thought the Universe would bring me all these amazing things and that our thoughts create our reality. I even had one ex-friend offer me a Jehovah Witness brochure she believed they could fix my wandering beliefs. I wasn't wandering, I wasn't lost! For the first time in all my life I'd been found.

My ex-friends made it apparent very quickly they weren't going to support me and became even more negative influences in my life. They thought I was selfish for wanting all these things and that it sounded like a cult. These friends showed their true colours eventually and it was a relief once they were out of my life for good. My family however chose to ignore these new-found beliefs of mine and I felt extremely alone. I wasn't recruiting people or forcing any of my beliefs on people, I just wanted someone to listen and support me through my awakening. This is why I turned to Facebook and joined many Law of Attraction groups in the hope of meeting like minded friends. I did meet quite a few actually who all have helped me greatly through the last few years of my life. It feels great to have like-minded friends across the world and I hope I'm lucky enough to meet them in person one day. Ema my Canadian friend is one of these people and I'm so grateful this gorgeous ray of sunshine was brought into my life. She taught me about myself, about love and that it's okay not to be accepted by people. I didn't need anyone's validation or support, I believed in myself and knew I could make all my dreams a reality and that's enough.

Once I started manifesting things into my life, crazy things started happening. My family could no longer deny the fact that what I was doing was extremely positive, it made me a better person and I was creating amazing things in my life. My parents now support fully what I do and even practice it a little themselves. It's completely changed the dynamics of our relationship and I'm glad they've changed their mindsets too. I am now surrounded by 100% support in my life for my spirituality and beliefs. As I've documented all the crazy and amazing manifestations that have happened to me in the last year of my life, it's impossible for anyone in my life to not join in! I love this quote I found online 'If you hang around me for too long, I'll brainwash you into believing in yourself and knowing you can achieve anything'. I live by this quote now and it's weird that my parents now come to me for advice instead of the other way round!

I constantly get asked by friends and even my parents how to manifest, how to be positive and how to change their lives around. So my advice to you, if your family or friends aren't supporting your journey is to be patient. You don't need anybody's validation and trust me as soon as they see the incredible results and manifestations that come into your life they'll all be knocking on your door asking for advice. A lot of people don't believe things until they see them and that's fine, but you don't have to live by that. The famous saying in the law of attraction is 'I'll see it when I believe it'.

It can be hard to feel uplifted and motivated constantly when you don't have that support unit around you, but for me my journey was to awaken these people and to attract like minded friends into my life. My journey has made the people around me awaken and do the Law of Attraction in their own lives. It's never been forced and it's surprising the amount of friends now who come up to me and thank me for showing them the light of the Universe.

Once I had fully awakened to who I was always meant to be, I soon realised why I had been given this journey and all the shit in my past. It was all to make me who I am today, a strong, independent woman who could heal and show others their inner power. Just call me superwoman? I'm joking. We all have these powers within us, we're brought here as either healers or teachers and I'm certainly a healer. That's not to say you can't be both either!

I've always been the go to person out of my friendship groups or work colleagues because of how wise I've always seemed. It's funny, I've never really classed myself as intelligent or smart but I just know about life. I can't tell you what the capital of Australia is or what the square route of 32 is but I can read people extremely well and just have a knowing about a lot of things. The one thing I've never had a knowing about is my own life. I've never asked any psychics whether they experience the same. Apart from my daughter, I've never known or seen sneak previews of my life before, only the odd gut feeling here and there. I'm known amongst my friends for having an impeccable talent for looking at couples and knowing if they'll last, for how long, and if they'll get married. Why I have this talent I'll never know, but I've never been wrong!

Since awakening I've learnt a lot about the messages I receive in odd and subtle ways. As awakened as I am, I do purposefully shut myself out of seeing and hearing messages because it simply scares the shit out of me! I'd rather just be Emma and get my gut feelings. I never understood why my YouTube videos on Law of Attraction started doing so well, they're now my most watched videos and you guys can't get enough of them! I'll be honest, they're my favourite to film and I love sharing my experiences with you. It's odd how someone simply sharing their experiences and life lessons can be appealing to so many, but then I realised that's exactly what I'm here for, to share the message.

My message is this book, my YouTube videos, my blog posts and everything I put my heart and soul in to. The Universe has given me this life and experiences to share them with you, so that you yourself can see your unlimited potential and continue to spread this message to even more people. My message is simple though, to be light, to give light and to love absolutely everyone. I believe love conquers all as cheesy as that may sound. I'll always remember the day I went to one of Tony Robbins' events in London last October, I'd never been before and I'd manifested these front row tickets worth £3,000 each for FREE! It was absolute fate that I was there that day and got my famous manifested hug from Tony Robbins. He picked me out of a crowd of over 3,000 people and helped me work through my blocks of finding Mr Right. I did say I wanted an Irish husband and he misheard me and thought I said I wanted a rich husband, god he must think I'm a gold digger! It was a life changing experience being stood next to my absolute idol, he had no idea how much he changed my life in the darkest days and here he was in person helping me once again.

I'd tweeted a picture of myself stood in front of the stage that morning and he even said "I saw that picture of you and you stood out from all the rest. You're special Emma".

Fuck, Tony Robbins had just made my year, no…my life! I felt so incredibly blessed to spend this time with him and I learnt so much about other incredible people he picked out from the crowd also. At the end of the tiresome ten hour day, we did a meditation practice to practise gratitude. We had to put our hands on our heart and feel it beating, think of every time we've smiled, laughed and cried and feel the gratitude in those moments. I tell you what it bloody works! The energy in that room was contagious. I really wish I could find a word to describe the pure peace and love I felt amongst these people. Not one person in that room judged, everyone just loved without question. We were all there for the same reason. By the end of the practice there wasn't one dry eye in the house and Tony came up to me and said "Everything happens for a reason." I don't know why I did what I did next, but I turned around and saw this lady stood two rows behind me not being hugged, she was sobbing her heart out and before I knew it I just embraced her and told her I loved her. This made both of us cry even more but she said thank you as that's what she needed to hear more than anything as she couldn't love herself. In that moment, in that woman, I learned my message. It was to tell as many people as possible that I love them, that the Universe loves them, the suffering inside can end and love conquers all. I even get emotional writing this now, because ultimately, I think that's what we all want to hear deep down.

That day changed my life forever and from that moment onwards I knew I had to shape my career and life path around this message. So I started filming more Law of Attraction YouTube videos. I told my followers, my friends, family and even strangers I loved them. From this I attracted so much more genuine love into my life and it felt incredible.

I started becoming more confident in my videos and voicing my beliefs and not being afraid of what people thought of me. For once in my career I wasn't Coupon Queen, I was Emma Mumford. You finally saw me, the real me and I developed connections with you all and set my soul on fire. Now because of this, I try to only do what sets my soul on fire so that I can still be Emma and help all of you see your fabulous potential. Due to very human things like bills and responsibilities, obviously I do still do things that don't set my soul on fire to earn money. This will one day be a thing of the past, and I know I will be spiritual full-time if that's even a career path? It's hard enough categorising a couponing business for HMRC, let alone a Spiritual Queen, but hell, if I can make a business out of coupons, I can make a successful business out of this!

I recently had a reading with Rachel, my psychic. I was going to include this in my 'What The Universe Told Me' chapter but I feel it fits in better here. My Mum and I went for a reading as my Mum was doubting her business venture and choices in life. My Nan was currently coming through to Rachel and she said "Look at what your daughter's done, everyone told her she couldn't do it and she said 'sod it' and look at her shine". I don't know why but hearing my Nan and even my Great-Nan who I'd never met, say this to my mum twice made me cry instantly. I do struggle to see my own worth sometimes still and even the scale of influence I have online. Hearing my relatives say this made me happy and fulfilled about how proud everyone up there was of me. I guess I've been so used to being mocked about what I do,

I needed to hear it from the Universe, I needed to hear it from the spirit world almost to validate that I could really be worthy of being a role model to people.

I always feel awkward when people put me on a celebrity pedestal because I'm not. Yes, I'm well known for my businesses and personality but I'm an everyday pizza-loving girl who just wants to help people shine. Rachel also said to me just how lovely my followers are as so many had booked in with her after my YouTube videos about her readings. She said it's very rare to continuously have positive lovely people follow one person but she said every single person couldn't stop singing my praises and were so positive and loving to Rachel. This means the message is working. I do feel such a sense of love for each and every one of my followers because you are simply amazing. All your comments, your well wishes, even your likes fill me up with a love I've never felt before. An unconditional accepting love of all I am, and all I share on my channels.

A light worker is someone who chooses to be a big light in this world. They choose to be the light, share the light and embrace the light into their own lives. We're all capable of being light workers and sharing the message amongst the world. The more people who do this, the more people it will reach. That's the fascinating thing about being born into this time, the power of social media and how the message can be shared millions of times around the world through the power of the internet, social media and apps. Through eBooks, real books, tablets, phones, computers and smart watches, we're all capable of acquiring data at the touch of a button, so sharing the message should be easy right? Well, it is slightly hard work when we live in a time where positive thinking and spirituality is still 'hippy shit'. We need to banish this old outdated Woodstock view of us light workers and show the masses, hey all we're doing is sharing the love, light and looking fabulous at the same time!

I first became a Light worker after reading Kyle Gray's 'Raise Your Vibration' last year. I called upon my Angels gang and took on this mission to share light amongst the world. Now this may sound super spiritual but being a light worker is really simple, you just need to make the commitment to yourself to be positive, to be the light and to share that light with others.

So many of us are light workers without even realising, I know I was! It's also important to honour how your body feels. Some days after a lot of reading, meditating and self-development I feel motivated and then minutes later feel like I could sleep for a thousand years. This is extremely normal and many laugh at me for taking power naps when I need them. This isn't me being unproductive or lazy, I'm simply honouring what my soul needs and that's rest.

Sometimes I don't even fall asleep, I lie in bed with my eyes closed and ideas, plans and inspiration come to me, then twenty minutes later boom, I'm full of energy again. Some days my body wants healthy food, other days it wants chocolate and all the unhealthy delights in this world. Once again I honour what my body wants. I eat when I want to and stop eating when I'm full. I used to be so concerned with my weight and calorie intake, now I simply give my body what it wants and I've never been so healthy (surprisingly!). I've also taken up yoga, running and dance classes at the gym as this new way of living has spurred me on to do more exercise. I think that's the absolute key to maintaining a healthy weight and manifesting weight loss is to simply be happy, and to make your body and soul happy also. It seems odd to tell you to eat whatever you want whenever you want but honestly it's worked for both myself and numerous other Law of Attraction advocates out there. Remember to act as if, if you were the ideal weight you would treat yourself, be happy and confident. So start doing that today and you'll manifest it a heck of a lot quicker.

I absolutely love running now, it never did anything for me before, but I now go for a morning run with some friends and it gets me in an incredible mind frame for the day ahead. I think what I love most about running is that it switches my mind off from work, in that moment all I can think about is my breathing, my legs and the beautiful countryside I'm running through. I love being amongst nature. I'm certainly a nature lover and love nothing more than sitting in a forest in the summer watching all the wildlife and world go past. Can you tell I was single for a year?

Yoga also helps me to focus and calm my mind and is one of my favourite things to do pre-running to stretch and gain energy. I now also have a gym membership (yup!) I go three times a week and really enjoy the dance classes I attend. Dancing is one of the things that does set my soul alight and always instantly uplifts me. It's funny, for ages

Selina and I were talking about dance classes to raise our vibrations and how we couldn't find any in the local area then boom we find Clubbercise and Dance Fitness. I've been doing these classes for around a year now and can honestly say I feel incredible, my body has never looked so smoking hot and yes I even manifested my bum coming back to me, it hadn't been seen since 2015! I never started any of this to lose weight or to tone up, I simply visualised my dream body and followed my intuition and had fun along the way. So get outdoors, get walking, running or whatever it is that sets your soul alight no matter how big or how small. These are also great stress relievers and you find 99.9% of the time most successful entrepreneurs work out every single day because it gives you incredible motivation, stamina and mindset. The key is to start off small, don't overload yourself with classes or activities or you'll probably end up giving up. Set goals and raise them every month just like you would with money or work.

I've got the book, the websites, the courses and the YouTube videos all available online for people to access, so why on earth did I start my own candle range? Well, I won't lie. I have always seen myself with a candle range as I'm a sucker for home decor. It was always inevitable amongst my friends and family that I would have my own candle range. I love candles because they always help me to relax within my home and de-stress. I love how they fill my home with fragrance and always look so inviting. So I wanted to create a law of attraction range, the first of its kind! I wanted these candles to reinforce the message, that you're doing awesome and I'm there in your living room motivating you to manifest your dreams! I wish I could be there in your homes motivating you personally but candles seemed like a much cheaper and more realistic option so I'm told.

Creating a sacred space in your home is so important as this will raise your vibration, and uplift you when you spend time at home. Seeing as I work from home and currently live by myself it was extremely important for me to have a safe, relaxing sanctuary which was productive for me but also a retreat where I can switch off. I did this by making my home me, I sage, I cleanse the space and have crystals displayed. I express my personality, my spirituality and have created a space of positive vibes for all who enter. So that's how I became one Spiritual Queen, fiercely achieving every single dream of hers!

Part II

How To Manifest

Law of

Attraction Queen

Whether you've never heard of the Law of Attraction before or you're an expert, covering and remembering the basics are so vital in your manifesting journey. I myself can even admit that even after years of practising and teaching this now, even I sometimes forget the basics. Essentially, the Law of Attraction is a belief that we can attract anything into our lives. It's all about having a positive and grateful mindset and being conscious to the belief that if we can see it in our mind we can hold it in our hands. Like attracts like - a bit like karma is the best way I can explain the Law of Attraction, what you put out into the world you get back. So for example, if you're being loving, kind, caring and happy you're going to attract lots of incredible miracles into your life including more love. If you're being negative, expecting the worst to happen and doubting everything guess what lovely your life isn't going to look too great. It can be hard at first to believe these concepts especially if you've been a negative person for quite some years. The key here is persistence and the dedication to yourself to create your dream life.

The Law of Attraction also teaches us that we are constantly speaking and thinking into existence - so wherever your energy goes it will manifest into your reality. This is great when you're positive and living the full Spiritual Queen life, but not so good when you're having a down day and just want to sit and play the victim. The Universe matches our standards, so essentially, we get what we tolerate in life. So if you've experienced some pretty shit things in your life and this book has been your wake up call, then darling it's time to raise your standards!

We all deserve our dream life, and I want to tell you for a fact that it is entirely possible - if you put the work in! Now for those of you who have absolutely no idea how to manifest your dream life here are my top techniques for manifesting. There are three famous steps in the Law of Attraction process - Ask, Believe, Receive. Now I'm going to blow that theory out the ball park and say, hun there are five. I've found since acknowledging these five steps it's made it so more enjoyable to manifest and most importantly easier!

1. Ask

The first step and most important is to ask the Universe, God, Source, Divine whatever you connect with for your desire. It's really important that you get specific and know exactly what it is you want. Now don't worry if you have absolutely no idea what it is you want in life, the Universe will soon help you out along the way. I always find that focusing on things that bring me joy is a great way to establish what I wanted in life. My love for helping people created my first money-saving business and now this one which helps people with spirituality and living their best life. You could even manifest simply being shown what your next step should be. You don't have to just manifest materialistic things, you can manifest emotions, answers and guidance galore! The way to ask the Universe can be simply by saying it out loud 'Universe I want to manifest my monthly salary increasing' I always like to add 'And so it is' at the end to see it as done. You only need to ask once for a manifestation, so whether you keep a goals list, say it verbally, write it down as an affirmation, think it, put it on a vision board this is ALL asking.

2. Believe

The second step is to believe that your desire will manifest at the perfect time. Now I know some of you will be saying "Well I just asked - how come my yacht, mansion and hunky husband aren't knocking at my door!" The answer is divine timing my dear. The Universe has a set timeline for you, and all will manifest at the exact right time. Enjoy that process too, it's no fun if you get everything at once, otherwise what would you focus on manifesting then? If you find it hard to believe that your desire can be yours, then ask for a sign. Connect to your Angels, spirit guides or simply the Universe and ask for a sign that your desire has been heard. Belief can take some time so make sure that you're doing your daily practises, working on your vibration and self-love in order to be in the best place possible to receive your manifestation.

3. Let Go

So this is the third step and an extra step I've added in - letting it go! This is a key part which most basic Law of Attraction methods skip past and is one of the most vital. Letting it all go. Now it may seem confusing that you should ask for your desire then forget all about it right? Crazy I know, but you actually make it happen so much faster when you let it go. So letting go means that essentially you're totally okay with both outcomes. If you want, need, become desperate over your desire then you're putting out a lack vibe and just like karma that's what you're going to attract back. Accepting that you believe it will manifest, but actually you're already really grateful for what you have now and surrender the outcome is an absolute game changer. This is the miracle, by seeing how far you've come, honouring your growth and not even needing the manifestation anymore. You do still hold that manifestation as your end goal, but you release how and when it will happen. By doing this you attract your desire so much faster and by living in the now, having fun and focusing on other things you let the Universe get to work!

4. Trust

Now again this is another important step which I've added in to the manifestation process. This is very similar to the believe step earlier, but I do think the two are separate. Once you've let go there will be a period where you're waiting for your manifestation to appear. This is when it's vital to trust the Universe's plan and witness your inner peace with the outcome. Acting as if essentially means you act as if you already have your desire. So if you wanted to manifest your dream man, you would date yourself, commit to yourself, take inspired action and become love. If you had your dream man you would be relaxed, feeling loved, and well getting on with your life. You wouldn't be sat in waiting on a text or feeling miserable. So really connect to the feelings you would have if your desire was here right now and live them now!

5. Receive

The last and final step is receiving your manifestation! YASSS now let the partying begin. You may receive signs, numbers or even intuition that your manifestation is on the way. I often sense something the day before it happens, if you do just relax and get excited baby! Honour your journey, thank the Universe and be grateful that your desire was brought to you. Share your story with others and help to bring the Law of Attraction into other people's lives too.

A key part to manifesting is to take inspired action. This does not mean you go out and force your dream man to be with you. We do not want you getting arrested for stalking! That's also not letting it go. Inspired action means showing up for yourself, so doing your daily spiritual practises, raising your vibration, if you're manifesting a job apply for them! Whatever it is show up to the Universe every day and take whatever actions you may need to take. While some situations may require you to be patient and take no action at all other than working on yourself, it does not mean be lazy. If you want to be a millionaire, you don't sit at home doing nothing. You work hard and find a way for that money to enter your life. If you feel like you've exhausted all your inspired action, then honour that. Take a step back and acknowledge that you've done all you can and now it's time to let go. It's in the Universe's hands and you can trust that.

Another great way to manifest is using vision boards. I love creating these and it's such a creative way to get clear about what you want in your life. You can also do these and get all the family involved and get creative. Where would you like to go on holiday? Where would you like to live? Stick lots of images on this vision board, be careful what you wish for though. I've heard numerous people actually attracting the house they put on their vision board so make sure what you put on there you actually want! You can also put words on your vision board, so any emotions you'd like to manifest i.e. love, happiness, joy. It's up to you where you want to store your vision board. Some people like to put them on the fridge, on their wardrobe or workspace. It's completely up to you. Personally I don't like to see mine everyday as I become too attached and don't end up letting it go! I store mine in my manifestation box.

A manifestation box is a shoe box that you design and make your own little Universe. I've covered mine with nice pictures and words that mean something to me. I created this manifestation box after I became so frustrated that I wasn't letting go of my manifestations by staring at them each day. I wanted a safe place full of great energy that could house my affirmations, vision board and any goals I had written down. So now it all goes in there and stays in my office. I believe that when I put my desires in this manifestation box that I let it go and the Universe is working on it for me. I don't need to worry about it and it's perfectly safe in my box. This works so well for me and I love having a sort through it every so often and ticking off and clearing all the manifestations that have happened.

I mentioned earlier about the importance of raising your vibration. Your vibes attract your reality, so if you're feeling negative, lacking or fearful, guess what you're attracting more of! Your vibration is super important to maintain and if vibration sounds like a weird word that makes no sense it basically means your vibes. So if you want to manifest your dream life, you need to work on maintaining a high vibe state so that you reflect what you want to manifest. The way you can do this is through EFT (Emotional Freedom Technique) and there are lots of great videos on YouTube for raising your vibration and for specific emotions. Brad Yates is my favourite teacher for EFT on YouTube. Looking after yourself, your health and removing any negativity from your life. Negativity can be the leading factor in our vibe being affected, so make sure you're not feeding the negativity and only putting energy into the positives. Watching your favourite movie, working on your self-love, all of these are great ways to lift your funks and raise your vibration. It is a daily practise though as your vibe will change depending on what happens in your daily life and thoughts.

So let's cover what you should be doing on a daily basis as part of your spiritual journey. There are certain tools and practises which will help to maintain your high vibe each day and will help you to incorporate gratitude into your everyday life. I personally love to do a gratitude practise each day, not only does this start my day off with love, it puts me in the best possible mood for the day ahead. I simply write five things I'm grateful for right now in my life. The way I like to do this is by writing 'I am so grateful for...because...' Some people confuse a gratitude practise for a manifestation list. Gratitude should simply be giving thanks for everything you have right now and these can be small or big things. If you find you're repeating the same points each day then really dig deep, what about your healthy organs, what about the clean water accessible in your tap, what about your vision right now to be able to read this book. There are so many things to be grateful for and I strongly urge you to make time for this practise each morning as soon as you wake up to put yourself in a great mood for the day.

I also like to do an EFT video each morning to raise my vibes, I dedicate half an hour every single day to my spiritual practices. They are so important and keep me connected to my faith in the Universe and feeling great in general. Law of Attraction isn't just a shower once and you're clean for your whole life kinda job, it's an everyday regime just like showering. The more you shower the more clean you are, just like gratitude. You can also write some affirmations in the morning as well to accompany your manifestations. So if you were wanting to attract money you could write 'I am constantly receiving money from unexpected sources'. Affirmations should always be written in present tense, even if they haven't materialised yet. You can say these out loud, write them down or even say them in the mirror for added effect. I like to stick my affirmations on my fridge so that every time I pass it I have to say them out loud and believe it!

There are lots of practises you can do for your morning routine, so go with what feels good for you. I know many people who just like to sit and meditate for fifteen minutes.

As long as you are dedicating time every single day to your spiritual practices you can't go wrong.

So what should you do if you're naturally a negative person and want to break this pattern? It's simple, know that life is happening *for* you not *to* you. All your past experiences, traumas, hurt and pain are all manifestations of your past thoughts and past beliefs. If that's not a big enough reason to make you wake up and think positively I don't know what is! At every given second, we are creating our reality with our words and thoughts so at first it will feel forced and will feel weird that you're having to tell yourself off for thinking negatively. The more you become aware of these thoughts and recognise them you can change them, witness them and own them. Remember that you create your reality so keeping your thoughts, vibes and words positive is in your best interest!

So where does the Law of Attraction originate from? It was first thought that hundreds of years ago it was taught to a man by the immortal Buddha. It is believed he wanted it to be known that 'What you have become is what you have thought. The mind is everything. What we think we become'. The Law of Attraction has been echoed throughout history with references in most religious texts. Even with such historical figures sharing their experiences with the belief such as Ghandi, Albert Einstein and Leonardo Da Vinci. The Law of Attraction has been argued to have always existed. Only now is it becoming more mainstream and widely known, as the world becomes ready to awaken. More and more of us are finding these teachings and sharing our light into the world. Even children being born now are being born with knowledge of past lives, spirituality and are already awakened. They are here to teach us, and I'm so blessed to have found the Law of Attraction at the age of twenty-two because now I can lead a life full of abundance and teach others this life-changing belief.

I really feel that the Law of Attraction is such an approachable way into spirituality. We all want to change our lives and manifest our dream lives, so what is not to love about that! Over the last few years since I've been doing Law of Attraction I have manifested some mind-blowing experiences that you will read throughout this book. Since finding the Law of Attraction and focusing on gratitude and positivity my life has opened up to such abundance and happiness. It truly is incredible what we can create with our minds and words.

One theme that I am continuously seeing though, is that at any stage of your journey we do forget the basics. Sometimes we're stuck in lack mentality and we keep ourselves from this wonderful abundance that wants to be in our lives. This is why I strongly suggest creating your own spiritual practise and committing to it each day, if you want your dream life you have to do the work. I'm not talking about vision boards or affirmations. I'm talking about being thankful each day for your life right now, working on yourself, making yourself happy, healing yourself and helping others. This is what doing the work means. The more you do the work the more the Universe will reward you with abundance in your life.

So what happens if you've done all of the above and your desire is still not manifesting? Well for example I had a client approach me for coaching sessions and she opened her email with 'I can't manifest anything!' Well as you can imagine my first response was of course, I'm not surprised if that's the story you keep telling yourself. So it's time to evaluate your behaviour up until this point.

Look at your thought patterns, are you certain of the outcome, relaxed, enjoying life, being carefree, are you positive about the future? Are you reflecting your desire, acting as if and allowing miracles to come to you? Have you been ignoring any intuition, niggling feelings or clear signs from the Universe? Normally, when manifestations aren't appearing even after a prolonged period of being calm and at peace with it, it can mean one of two things. One is divine timing, there is always free will at play here, so we may have a window of opportunity open for this manifestation, but others may not be actioning their intuition or maybe missing signs. The Universe allows free will, but eventually if someone ignores a feeling for too long the Universe will step into action and give a loud wake up call. I mean that in the best way possible, but it really will put you or someone else involved on that right path through force. I also want to add that especially if you're manifesting a specific person romantically or not, that again free will plays into accord here and sometimes it's just not for our highest good for it to materialise. I tried to manifest my ex-boyfriend back when I first found the Law of Attraction and THANK GOD the Universe didn't make that happen because there was so much more happiness waiting for me in my dream man. The Universe knew what the best option was for me.

Secondly, it could be down to you and your vibe. It's time to get honest at this point as it's only going to benefit you in the long run. When a negative thought comes into your head, how do you address it? The best way in my opinion is to send it love, I simply say 'Ego, I know you're trying to protect me but don't worry I've got this'. Even if your situation seems helpless right now, you can change that in an instant. Do you still feel like a victim? Many times, especially when manifesting love, we have to own our emotions and choose to take ourselves out of victim mode and into success mode. We need to re-write the story we tell ourselves and life as if it's already here. So by re-claiming our power, choosing love, forgiving those who have done wrong to us even if they haven't apologised to us directly, we set ourselves free and allow ourselves to be present, able to stand in our power and be fearless about the future. Because all we have is right now, we can't go back to yesterday and tomorrow hasn't happened yet - so choose how you want to feel right now and live that with every ounce of your soul.

One problem I hear time and time again is that people will use the Law of Attraction to manifest something - get it and stop everything. Then they wonder why abundance isn't consistently flowing to them. Well I think the answer is straight forward here - like attracts like. If you want consistent abundance and miracles each day of your life you're going to need to show up every day of your life. This means doing your daily practices, finding gratitude in each moment, using affirmations, raising your vibration and committing to your journey. The more consistent you are the more consistent the Universe will be with you. It may seem simple but I promise it's much easier to pull yourself out of a funk when your consistently doing these practices instead of once in a blue moon.

Another great tip for your Law of Attraction toolkit is to cleanse your home. As well as taking care of ourselves and vibes we need to take care of the vibes within our home. Our workplace and home are most likely to be where we spend most of our time. So these spaces need to reflect that love and tranquillity we wish to see within ourselves. Cleansing these spaces can be really easy and powerful - I personally like to use white sage and paulo santo sticks. If you don't like the idea of burning these as white sage can be a bit stinky, a cleansing spray can also be just as beneficial. Have a look at some aura or cleansing spray's and use these around your home, work space and even on yourself to clear negative energy. You can even take these away with you on holiday or if you travel regularly to cleanse your hotel room and create a scared space of good vibes.

The key I find to the Law of Attraction which so many people forget is - the answer is always within us. It's so easy for us to search externally for an answer through psychics, oracle cards the lot and I don't think there's anything wrong with that. The problem stems when like me I became almost addicted to this. I valued these psychics predictions more than my own intuition. I was becoming reliant on an external force to rule my life which just makes no sense and is completely disempowering ourselves. Every now and again we may need a little encouragement or to ask the Universe something but we are all capable of doing this - it just takes practise. Learn to trust yourself and remember that we have the power to shape our future's. If you want an incredible life then you can manifest that - no psychic in the world can tell you any differently. If you believe something will happen trust that and honour that feeling. The more you honour and listen to your intuition the more the connection will grow and you will be able to recognise the signs to listen to.

We all have it where we may be empathic, or a good judge of character all of this is intuition and should be listened to. I'm sure we've all had moments in our life where we say 'I knew that was going to happen!'. This is your intuition speaking loud and clear baby. So instead of searching for and seeking answers externally - trust yourself, reclaim your power and know that at the end of the day only you know your true destiny and can manifest it into your reality.

Finding My
King Queen

Manifesting your twin flame is probably one of the hardest, yet the most rewarding of manifestations. A twin flame is not just a soulmate. We do however travel around in groups of soulmates. These can be your friends, pets, family, children, they can be absolutely anybody in your life. A twin flame is different, it's your mirror image or 'the one' essentially. You can only have one twin flame and you can certainly get false twin flames also. My second ex was certainly a false twin flame but he was sent to deliver me to my future.

In August 2016, after having my heart utterly shattered by my ex, I decided no more bullshit. I didn't want this to happen yet again. I didn't want any more meaningless bullshit. I wanted the one, my husband, happiness. I knew what I wanted in life, why wasn't I getting it? I remember powerfully, on my twenty-third birthday, my mum wrapped my presents in white butterfly wrapping paper; this was one of the many white butterfly signs, which I'll get to. With this in mind I decided on my wish as I was blowing out my candles, and it was that on my twenty-forth birthday I'd be with my husband and surrounded by loving friends. That wish certainly came true. From that moment on, I shaped my future and the Universe heard loud and clear that I wasn't messing around anymore.

I've never really been attracted to white butterflies in particular. I was never really a butterfly kind of girl. One day a few days after my ex had left the flat in the April, I started seeing them everywhere, groups of them, stalking me almost every single day. My friends at the time thought I was absolutely nuts until they themselves witnessed that everywhere I was, white butterflies followed. I knew this was a sign from the Universe, but at the time I did believe it was to do with my ex. Months passed and these bloomin' white butterflies kept stalking me, what on earth did they mean! Eventually, I decided it must just be a sign that I'm on the right path. I'd also asked the Universe to play me Coldplay songs randomly every time I was on the right path.

So after my twenty-third birthday I decided it was about time the Universe listened up to what I wanted and that I wasn't going to settle for anything less than freakin' amazingness! I remember fiercely saying "Universe, I want my husband please, no more meaningless boyfriends. It's all or nothing now, show me what you've got!". Sadly he didn't just appear in the room after that powerful intention I'd set, he didn't miraculously appear at all for another nine months. I always knew I'd meet the one young, I knew he'd be older than me and I wanted him to be the mirror image of me.

I then spoke to my friend Ema in Canada who was extremely excited that I'd set this intention. She suggested writing a dream man list and getting extremely specific. Ema's Mum had been doing the Law of Attraction for decades and had taught Ema everything she knew. Ema was a fantastic help throughout this process, helping me every step of the way and getting me to be extremely specific in what I wanted so that only the best showed up! Ema also advised that I buy two of things, and only get artwork of couples, never have a person by themselves. I had read this theory online about how you should put two toothbrushes out, empty half the wardrobe and to sleep on your side of the bed, all to allow this person into your life. This all seemed a bit too much hassle for me. I did try it out for a month but then realised I had too many clothes and that Mr Right would have to accept I need a walk in wardrobe not a shared IKEA wardrobe in my flat. I did however buy love quotes to put around the house and actively liked statuses on Facebook all about love and couples and scrolled past any that celebrated singleness etc. I even changed my relationship status on Facebook to 'married', this did confuse a few people but by that point everyone expected this from me! It was only recently I realised I'd left it as married so I have now changed it to 'In a relationship'. On my dream man list I wrote everything from hair colour, height, job, hobbies, personality traits and places we'd visit together. I folded up this dream man list and put it into my manifestation box in my office, to forget all about it, and let go. I knew what I was seeking had been seeking me for a lot longer than I had realised.

Letting go of the outcome can sometimes be the hardest part of manifesting. How could I simply 'let go' of wanting this husband? Months passed and I just felt helpless some days, I'd see all these happy couples and think why can't I have this? My ex had got his girl, why couldn't I be happy after everything I'd been put through?

Around Christmas time I did feel lonely, I did feel at an all-time low being surrounded by love and all the festiveness. It's just not the same when you're single. I remember going in to Pandora with one of my friends and seeing the new rose gold collection. I instantly fell in love with a beautiful ring, which funnily enough looked like an exact replica of my dream engagement ring I'd even stuck on my vision board months ago. I had read somewhere that some women had actually bought engagement rings and worn them on their wedding finger and manifested their husbands that way. Well I was up for trying anything at that point and did absolutely love this ring. I decided to wear it on my middle finger though, but it is still on my left hand at least! I've now worn this ring for nearly two years and still wear it every day. Do I think this helped me manifest him? Maybe. I can't say for certain but I think it was a clear indication to the Universe that I wanted that ring on my finger at some point!

We were now into the New Year and still no sign of Mr Right. I had completely become bitter about it by then. I was so disheartened that I'd nearly been single for a year, that no men were ever interested in me and that no matter what I did he wasn't coming anytime soon. I also knew deep down he wouldn't appear until I'd been single for a year. Big manifestations always take a year to appear for me and this felt so far away at this point. I'd had my reading with Rachel my psychic in the January, and this is where she said I'd meet him, this year and it would be after my holiday with a dear friend of mine. Great I had no holidays booked at that point, how bloody long was this guy taking!

In the April, I then had a soulmate reading with another psychic. After hearing all about Mr Right and what our future holds I certainly felt a massive shift in energy. In the reading as we were video calling, a white butterfly circled him and I thought here we go! The psychic said "He's here!" That was Mr Right's energy. He had been sending me these white butterflies for the last year, even before I set the intentions of wanting a husband, to show me he was on his way and thinking of me. Mr Right had showed up every time I needed him, even if he couldn't be with me in the psychical at this point. Now if that's not romantic I don't know what is! He had been seeking me well before I'd even asked for him. Also in all honesty I'd given up by that point, it had been so long and a year now since I'd been single I just wasn't fussed anymore. I knew he would arrive at some point but I was so happy with myself and my life at this stage I wasn't in any rush to meet him! I believe this is what helped me manifest him so quickly after this reading because I had fully let go and accepted it was on its way.

With this new found energy, I could really sense something was going to happen soon. I had the idea of July in my head so didn't really worry much about how it would happen as I had ages right? Well actually, little did I know I only had four weeks left of being single. I really did enjoy being single towards the end, I had finally learnt to be independent, happy and had finally found myself. I had amazing friends and family around me, I remember thinking god can he just wait a bit longer because I'm really enjoying this life!

I then went to Barcelona on holiday with my friend and had the palm tree moment Rachel had spoken about. It was odd, although I had this moment and recognised it, I didn't suddenly think oh well here comes Mr Right! I was super relaxed about the whole thing, something which baffled me as I had been so desperate for so long. I was finally at peace with myself and being single. My single friends and I decided that we should start dating ourselves instead. We knew we wanted to attract these men but were all self-employed and super busy. How would we even have time for these men to enter our lives?

So every Friday night we would go out for a meal, to the cinema and date ourselves. I would also buy myself flowers as they made me happy and would treat myself to a back massage at the spa and pamper myself regularly all to help my self-love. Having this love and respect for myself was so important and still is, as the saying goes if you can't love yourself, you can't love anybody else. I truly needed to find this love for myself and everything in my life to awaken me and be the person I was meant to be for my Mr Right.

After my reading, which confirmed the white butterflies to me, I knew I wanted to get a white butterfly tattooed on my wrist to symbolise him and my journey. I booked in with my lovely friend Natalie who's done most of my tattoos. Natalie asked the meaning behind the tattoo so I explained, as a fellow Law of Attraction junkie Natalie found this story amazing and in that moment I said "Wouldn't it be funny if I met my husband tomorrow!". Well as I've learnt with all my big manifestations this is a very powerful and very fulfilling phrase of mine because low and behold I actually did meet him the very next day! It's so odd but amazing how all of this played out.

So on Saturday 20th May 2017, I went to Bournemouth (a town in the south of England) for the day shopping with Selina. We had a fantastic day out together and it just felt like a very average day. We then returned home and my other single friend group messaged to ask if we were doing a date night tonight as we missed our usual Friday night. I really couldn't be bothered, I was so tired from shopping all day, the thought of sitting in my pjs on the couch, watching TV with chocolate sounded ideal. Only problem was there was no food in the house, so driven by my stomach I reluctantly said yes. We decided to go to the local Brewhouse pub, which was really unlike us as we always went elsewhere for food. We'd actually been to the Brewhouse pub for the first time the Friday previously for date night and we got speaking to the band and I could almost feel like I needed to be in that pub so I said to my friend I'm going to ask for a sign. I didn't get a sign until we went on to another pub for a drink. As we walked in the band were playing my favourite Coldplay song! I knew something was about to happen. My friends picked the Brewhouse that night and I thought I'm meant to be here. So all three of us sat at a table of four and ordered some delicious burgers.

I don't actually remember at what point he walked in and sat down with his friend next to us. I just remember suddenly looking around and seeing this guy staring at me. So as you do, I stared back. I said to my friends there was a hot guy over there staring at me and, as your friends do, they all turned round at the same time to look, not obvious at all! All night we kept exchanging looks and smiles. I said to the girls "Why isn't he coming over if he likes me?" I'll be honest as flattered as I was, I wasn't there to meet anyone so I simply got on with eating and chatting to my friends.

About two hours had passed by now and at this point I was frustrated, I couldn't understand why this guy kept looking at me and not doing anything about it! We were about to leave when his friend turned around and asked us the best places to visit in Dorchester (our home town). Great conversation starter! My friends knew this was a sign and immediately said "Come and join us!" Thanks guys, now two random men were sat with us. Seeing him closer up, I did fancy him more and he certainly seemed interesting. My two friends were sat closest to him. I was sat on my phone not paying any attention. I just had no interest what so ever about meeting someone, I must have looked so rude! After about an hour of chatting we realised it was midnight and probably should all get going.

My friend had invited them to our pub quiz we go to every week and of course that gave him an opportunity to ask for my number. For once without thinking I actually gave a stranger my real number! I'm always careful who I give my number out to because of my line of work, but again it didn't feel like I was in control here the Universe was making this happen whether I liked it or not! That evening I remember going to bed literally thinking nothing of this encounter, little did I know who I had just met. The next day he text me and I remember that's when I started getting excited and feeling butterflies in my stomach, I started telling my friends I'd met someone, that he was texting me and everyone literally started freaking out with excitement. Everybody around me kept saying "This is him!" and I was like I'm just texting a random guy can everyone stop buying wedding outfits please! I have no idea why I wasn't even excited at this point. We grew very close very quickly through texting and he did come to the pub quiz the next week. He's since explained to me how cold I was at the quiz and he thought I didn't like him because of this encounter but for me I didn't know how to date, or how to show a guy I'm interested. I wanted to take things slow, but clearly that came across as not interested to him thanks to my impeccable dating experience!

After a few meetings, he eventually asked me out on a date! Holy fuck, Mumford was going on a date with a real life hot man. What on earth would I wear to this life-changing meal and oh god my Bridget Jones underwear collection would certainly have to be burnt. It was time to get myself back in the dating game. This is where my ego decided to kick in big time and I started self-sabotaging. Everything about him was so perfect, everything I'd asked for but I hadn't taken the time to find that out yet. I was so quick to rule him out because I didn't know much about him and I was scared, really scared to let someone in and well meet the husband I'd been asking for over the last year.

I think it suddenly dawned on me, the reality of what I had just manifested. Could he be the one? Was I ready to give up single life? Was this even what I wanted anymore? All of these questions kept going around and around in my head, it was suffocating and really threw me into a low vibration. I remember my friends saying they'd seen me at my absolute happiest and my darkest all in the space of a week. One minute I would be happy and want everything with him, the next I'd throw it all away. There were three occasions I told him I didn't want to continue this and to stop messaging me. The first time I had a freak out I felt relieved that I didn't have the pressure of this anymore, I remember that night I went to bed and had the most vivid dream. I was surrounded by Angels and they all kept repeating "message him now" it felt urgent, like my life depended on it, I felt so forced to do this. I sat bolt upright in bed, I looked at the clock and it was 4am. I text him apologising for what I'd said and that I was wrong. In my sleep-deprived and restless state when texting him, I also ended up accidentally Facetiming him, good one Mumford great way to make yourself look desperate! Clearly being cool and subtle was not one of my many talents.

After this freak out I actually told him exactly what I had been manifesting, that I was looking for a husband and nothing else. I explained this is why I was freaking out because I wasn't sure and I didn't know what to do. Really I can't play it cool! To my surprise he completely understood and agreed that he was looking for exactly the same things as I was and to settle down. What a relief, he doesn't think I'm crazy! This helped me to realise that sometimes we don't know instantly whether someone is the one, it takes time. I think in my head I always had the idea that Mr Right would just waltz in and be like "Hey wife, let's go and live happily ever after." In reality it did not happen like that at all. There were also a lot of external reasons for my caution to do with his past, it was scary to put my trust in a guy I'd just met but I did just trust him. The third freak out was the hardest, by this point I felt emotionally ruined. I was so up and down and this time I had to stay away until his past had been dealt with. I remember just having a numb pain inside. I just felt like someone had kicked me in the gut, I was miserable. I felt like I couldn't breathe properly and all I wanted to do was be in his arms. Within days I just couldn't hack being apart from him any longer. Being with him was as easy as breathing, being without him felt like I was constantly suffocating. By this point I realised I needed to stop fighting, stop putting up barriers and resisting my destiny.

The first time we kissed I certainly felt the Universe was at work. I didn't expect him to try and kiss me but here we were stood in my kitchen after a lovely meal together in Bath (a beautiful town near by). In that moment I didn't think, I kind of froze and I felt something push me from behind, it felt like the Universe was pushing me into him and it did feel amazing. After that moment I knew exactly who he was. It was only hard because I was resisting, if I had trusted my gut and let it be I would have had a much smoother ride. These freak outs did make us closer though, so although painful I'm glad they happened. We are extremely close now and I do feel that I can tell him anything and be my completely crazy self around him.

I remember finding my dream man list a few weeks after meeting him, I went through it and he was about 80% of the list. This did worry me as with the Law of Attraction you're taught to not settle for any less than 100%. One of my lovely followers Debbie really helped me out here, she explained how her husband wasn't everything on her list straight away, you have to learn these things about them and discover the traits. Low and behold within months he had gone up to 98% where he currently stays, not bad at all though!

The only things he doesn't tick is spiritual and have a love of photography. Truthfully, I only wrote the love of photography down because of my job. He's going to take a lot of photos of me for my work so he kind of has to like it really! He doesn't mind doing this though and is actually quite good, so really I'm not bothered by this at all now.

Spirituality I guess was an important trait for me because of how much I live and breathe it. I needed someone to support me, listen to me and equally believe in the things I do in order to uplift me. I've been mocked, made fun of and laughed at for all I do spiritually, so having someone who sees the things I do and believes in the power of positivity is important. A psychic once told me, apparently I will be the one to awaken him so watch this space who knows, but 98% is pretty amazing anyway and I'm happy with that.

It turns out when I asked him, he had thought of a dream woman list also, he hadn't written it down sadly but he did say that I was what he'd asked for too. Due to a psychic's powerful description of this confident, spiritual husband I did start to doubt him. No matter how much I tried to think positively and just believe what will be will be, this doubt in my mind kept creeping back in. I reluctantly booked in another reading with this psychic. I remember the week leading up to it I kept thinking, what if he tells me this isn't Mr Right, what am I going to do? It was July 4th when I had my reading with this psychic again and straight away he said there is a reason why we're having this reading today after several delays either end. It was a day of celebration especially in America where he's from and he said the Universe is celebrating the fact you've found him! I can't begin to tell you the relief I felt when he said these words.

For weeks I'd been so worried that I'd fallen for the wrong person and I did know deep down really that the Universe had delivered him to me all along. The psychic gave me such a beautiful second reading and even said we will hardly ever argue but when we do it will just awaken him even more. Now that's what I like to hear! I should say, I do believe he has the potential to be spiritual. He is extremely positive and we do mirror each other a lot, so it would be impossible for him not to have the potential to awaken. Good things come to those who wait and for now I'm happy with him being himself and where our relationship is going.

There have been many weird coincidences throughout our time together so far, we have so much in common and like I said we are mirrors of one another. For one of our first big dates he surprised me with tickets to see Coldplay in Cardiff. So on the 11th June 2017 I was off to Cardiff, it suddenly dawned on me that I had manifested all of this. Last July, my friend from London had offered me a ticket to see Coldplay as someone had dropped out. I instantly said yes and was ready to transfer the money. I had to see this tour as it had all of my favourite manifestation and positive songs in. Sadly, the ticket fell through and it was given to someone else. I was left gutted that I was so close to seeing my all-time favourite band. I remember in that moment saying "I will see this tour within the next year and I will go with my dream man." Well, little did I know the Universe was going to make that happen! So there I was stood in Principality stadium in Cardiff with Chris Martin in front of me, my dream man to the left of me and I was at the 'Adventure of Lifetime' tour. When they played Yellow I tried so hard not to burst in to tears, I had no idea they'd play this song and this was the song that randomly kept playing to me every time I was on the right path. I never really liked the song Yellow but it kept finding me and here it was again confirming to me everything was bloody fantastic in my life. The lyrics speak so loudly to me and when Chris sung "Look at the stars, look how they shine for you, and everything you do" it felt like this was the Universe saying hello and showing me just how powerful I really am in that moment.

Another powerful manifestation with Mr Right was our first holiday together. Very quickly into our relationship we knew we wanted to go away together for my birthday. We got quite a few quotes from a great travel agent I use a lot. We didn't know where we wanted to go but Santorini kept popping up in the quotes. Sadly, it was out of our budget and I was gutted about this. I'd always wanted to visit Santorini and take beautiful photos of the stunning landscapes.

After numerous quotes we just couldn't decide on a location, nothing felt right to me. I gave up, I said to the Universe that night "I want to go to Santorini for £500", and I let go. I gave up on having to go away for my birthday and went to sleep. The next morning I went on a run with my friend and she was suggesting various places to look at, again I just didn't feel motivated anymore. I returned home and checked my emails and at 11:11am (a very spiritual number) Angela from the travel agents had emailed me a quote for Santorini over my birthday for only £542. I instantly sent it to Mr Right knowing this was a sign, he didn't reply as he was at work. I eventually got a reply hours later saying it looked good. Angela called me up saying "Emma the price has just dropped to £501, this never happens, you have to book this now!" I took this as a clear sign from the Universe that this was meant to happen and booked it without even asking Mr Right. It was a tense moment as I thought this could have started our first ever argument, but luckily half an hour after booking the holiday, he text me to say "Book it!" I was clearing out my manifestation box one evening and came across a piece of paper that said "Go to Santorini with Mr Right in 2017" well boom thank you Universe!

In less than a year I've manifested everything I'd ever asked for, a happily ever after with the perfect person. It still makes me feel emotional now because I'm just so grateful that we live in an incredible world where this is possible. We can create our lives and fill them with incredible loving things. So my advice to you if you're trying to manifest your dream love is to get specific and make it so damn clear to the Universe that you're not settling for anything less than perfection. Make a commitment to yourself, date yourself and work on your self-love. In order to manifest we need to match our desires, if you want someone spontaneous become spontaneous yourself! Looking back, a year did seem like a long time to be single, but I needed it. I needed it to awaken, to grow, to become the person I am and to perfect everything within me to become the best version of myself for Mr Right. All the pain, the struggles and hardship was all worth it now I get to wake up next to my Mr Right who fills me with so much genuine happiness and love. All of it was worth it to have him here with me now and forever more.

Money Queen

For a while now I haven't really been focusing on manifesting money, I've just let it flow to me naturally. I used to be so focused on how much I'd earn a month and this was great but also it didn't allow me to let go and allow an unlimited flow come to me as I was limiting what I wanted to manifest.

I first learnt how to manifest money two years ago after breaking up with my ex-boyfriend. I was left to pay our rent on the flat, and at the time of signing up I was only earning enough to pay half. I never thought I'd be in a situation where I'd have to pay the rent all by myself. After finding the Law of Attraction I knew this would be the answer to my money prayers, I knew it was possible to manifest my income increasing no matter how hopeless the situation may have seemed at the time. My family didn't put much pressure on me, and I didn't put that pressure on myself. I knew I was going to be okay after everything I'd been through the Universe has my back.

Within six months I had manifested tripling my annual turnover in my business, so not only could I afford to live in my flat and lead a great life - I could manifest a house with a garden and be able to afford it by myself. The best thing about this was, I didn't do anything different in my business, I still did exactly the same work as I was before, but it was just earning an incredible amount more! I think what really helped me do this so successfully was to believe that the Universe had my back, knowing I'd be supported and that I wouldn't be made homeless and knowing that I always had my family's support if I needed it. I had options no matter what, and that's what released the control and pressure off the situation.

The ways in which I manifested this money and all the money I've earned since was by one, watching Jim Carey being interviewed by Oprah many years ago. Jim spoke about writing a cheque to himself for $10 million dollars and gave himself five years to earn this through acting. He did of course achieve this within the five years so this is how I first got inspired. I wrote myself a cheque from my actual bank account's cheque book for £1,000,000 and gave myself five years to achieve this. I'm now two years into that manifestation and although it still feels a long way off I'm working through any blocks that come up and successfully growing my businesses at a steady rate.

By writing the cheque, placing it in my purse and also writing this goal on my fridge, every time I went to the fridge or looked in my purse I would feel the abundance of being a millionaire. I've always sensed that I would be really successful in my businesses although the thought of being a millionaire excited me, now I'm more disconnected from my ego, I realise that as long as my needs and my family's needs are met then I'm already a millionaire in abundance! The key to manifesting money is to accept and explore that money can come from multiple sources, it doesn't JUST have to be your monthly salary or by winning the lottery.

By realising that ALL money comes from the Universe you will notice how it magically appears in the most unexpected places. Now with my money-saving background I was used to never paying full price and getting discounts galore. Even as a Blogger I would be sent free products to review - all of these are money from the Universe. Although it's not money coming into your account, it's money staying in your account. So I started getting my favourite brands gift me products I would buy week in week out and loved already, the best partnerships were when they would pay for a feature on top of the freebie! I started attracting discount codes on everything and even strangers handing me coupons in shops to save on the item I was buying. This was the best manifestation having absolute strangers come up to me and say 'Hey I have a spare 35% off code you can use at the till'. Thank you Universe and thank you kind souls.

Really money is just an exchange of services, so by realising that coupons, discounts, freebies are ALL ways of manifesting money by allowing your actual hard earned money to stay in your bank account. See there was a reason the Universe wanted me to be Coupon Queen first of all! You can also manifest money through family members, maybe they could gift it to you spontaneously. I know a few people feel bad when this happens, but it's key to remember that they wouldn't be gifting it to you unless they wanted to and knew they could attract more as well. It doesn't matter who this money comes from, it's coming from the Universe where there are no limits.

I also used the new moon as a powerful way to manifest. The new moon is the manifesting moon, so you don't just have to manifest money you can focus on all of your manifestations for the month ahead. I would print off a 'Magic Check' from Rhonda Bryne's *The Secret* website and fill out my cheque for the month ahead. Every single month when writing these cheques and my goals down on a new moon they would manifest. So if you want to increase your monthly income whether you're self-employed or employed, get writing your cheques and goals on the new moon.

Another practise I love to manifest money into my life is doing EFT (Emotional Freedom Technique) videos and saying affirmations out loud. I personally love Brad Yate's 'Money Magnet' video on YouTube. Every time I do this video I manifest money in a really unexpected way. A new client will get in touch, a new brand will want to work with me. I'll get an overpayment, yes you can manifest being overpaid too, and not having them claw it back! You can also repeat the affirmation daily *'I'm a money magnet, and money finds me irresistible'*. Affirmations are so important as what we say and think becomes our reality. I personally love to use the affirmation *'Money continues to flow to me easily through unexpected sources and in unexpected ways'*. Now saying these affirmations daily will really get you manifesting money quickly!

Another great way to manifest money I've found is by donating to charities. I've always loved raising money for charities by doing sponsored runs and challenges. I'm so passionate about helping charities in the best way I can. Now that I'm surrounded by abundance, I feel it's important for me to give back and help the Universe's mission. So I always make time each month to donate what feels good to a charity of my choice. I don't do this to purposefully manifest more money, I stumbled upon this technique by wanting to give back to the community and by feeling good about using my abundance to help those in need. Always give what you feel comfortable with parting with each month and what makes you feel abundant. Just know that what you give to help others even if it's just your time, will come back to you tenfold.

I get asked frequently in my coaching sessions, how can they act as if, if they literally can't go out and treat themselves? I love this question because the answer is easier than most expect it to be. Acting as if isn't going out and putting a load of splurges on your credit card or spending your last hard earned cash on feeling abundant and then not eating for the week. Acting as if is ALL about the feelings, yes you can take inspired action and yes you should treat yourself but if you can't you need to honour that. Otherwise you'll end up in a heap of negativity and resentment about treating yourself which isn't going to manifest anything. The secret to acting as if is to reflect what you'd be like when you receive your abundance. So if you had plenty of money you'd be calm, happy, loving life, focusing on other areas of your life and these are the emotions you need to focus on. One of my clients was off up to London and wanted to go into Harrods to see how the rich acted and be amongst wealth. I agreed that this was a really good idea and that she should buy something. Nothing big that would make her feel uncomfortable, simply something that made her feel good. I always advise treating yourself to things that feel good NOT things that are expensive. In the end she bought herself a chocolate bar from Harrods and came away feeling more abundant, rich in life and she had a chocolate bar for the way home!

Another trap I fell into with money was wanting to be debt free. I visualised paying off my ex's debts for good and being free of my past. That debt wasn't even my fault, but it was my responsibility to pay it off now and the Universe would reward me for this. Instead of feeling like a victim, I accepted my reality and just had faith that this money would be returned to me. I manifested the exact amount in a month to become debt free, yet when the money was paid into my account I didn't pay the debt off. I paid 80% off. Why? I have no idea! I wanted to keep this hard earned money and couldn't quite part with it as it was paying off someone else's debt. After six months of sitting on this money, and still feeling no better as I still got letters from my debt collectors and still had my past looming over me, I thought fuck it! I didn't need that money, it was just sat in my account, it was all ego wanting that bank balance when I'd manifested it to clear my debt. I straight away called up the debt collectors and paid it off in full. I can't tell you the relief I felt after that phone call knowing I was finally financially free. I felt abundant and free at last knowing I could finally move forward. The Universe did reward me greatly. Not only did I get all that money back, but during that time I had occurred two defaults on my credit file because my ex wasn't making regular payments to my account for his debt. Here in the UK your credit file updates every six years. So, I should have had these two defaults on my account for another three years, however when speaking to a mortgage advisor a few months later thinking I had absolutely no hope with my credit, he said 'Emma they're gone, there's nothing on your credit file it's perfect!' Thank you Universe.

Comparison is an easy trap to fall into especially with money, we are surrounded by celebrities and influencers all parading they're cash around online. We all want their lifestyle let's admit it, but does it really make them happy? I used to look at celebrities and entrepreneurs thinking I was different to them. The truth is there is nothing different between us, we are all an expression of love. When fame is removed, money and all materialistic possessions we're all the same - we're souls having a human experience. Most celebrities do the Law of Attraction so it's no surprise they lead they're dream lives, they've just been doing it a bit longer than we have. So instead of feeling envious or judging them, I now applaud them and think that will be me one day. I'll have the lush house overlooking the sea, I'll have a nice car and jet set around the world. We can have anything in this life so remember don't separate yourself from your idols because once upon a time they were probably right where you are now. When they started out they had dreams, visions of success and did all of these steps you're taking right now. So see them as an example that your success will come too.

Now, I want to discuss the shady side of spirituality and money. Through my own Law of Attraction journey, I've learnt there are a lot of con artists in the self-help genre. They promise you results, they guarantee your manifestations happening. The truth is no one can guarantee you anything. I got approached by a client looking to take coaching sessions and she asked me 'What results do you guarantee?' I replied 'None. All of the results come from your commitment to your journey and your effort each day. I can guarantee

however, that I will support you and give you great tools
I feel suit your needs'. I didn't hear back from her, why?
Because I couldn't guarantee her the dream man, the dream
house, the dream anything. She didn't see that no one
can give us these things no matter how much money we
spend, the answers are always within us. I see so many big
influencers in the self-help scene who prey on this logic, that
if you invest in yourself (buy their course, books, DVDs,
seminar tickets) the Universe will reward you greatly, so
spend thousands out of desperation in the hopes the Universe
will return it!

This never works, because you're not seeing your worth truly,
the only person you're investing in is the speaker. Now I'm
all for supporting great teachers, you will see how many
great authors and teachers I mention in this book. I buy their
books and content for sure, but it's out of choice and they
have never pressured me or taken advantage of me to buy
their content out of desperation.

I've always carried these morals into my own work, I never
pressure or convince people to buy my work. Investing in
yourself isn't spending money when it doesn't feel good. I
would much rather people watch all my free content online
as that is showing up for yourself also. Yes, I have bills to pay
and if I want to do this full-time I do need to earn money,
but the right people will always find my work. I would never
want anyone buying into my work out of desperation and
fear, because that doesn't make either of us feel great. So
please don't be fooled by the shady side of spirituality, the
best and authentic teachers will always have free content

online as well as paid content which they won't have to force you to buy because you will feel comfortable and happy investing in that when the time is right. Not to manifest more money out of desperation.

After successfully manifesting money over the last few years, I'd hit a point recently after launching my spiritual business full-time where I had no idea how much I was earning in either businesses. I feel this was out of fear. My Extreme Couponing business had been slowing down as I turned my focus elsewhere and with Facebook always changing their algorithms, it's becoming harder to reach your audience meaning money had slowed down. I was avoiding this because of my business sale and having just gone full-time with my spiritual business I thought I was lacking. When writing this chapter, I felt called to actually sit down and work out what I've earned over the last month in both businesses. To my surprise I was earning near enough exactly the same but just in two businesses now instead of one. It was amazing to see how far my spiritual business had come in only six months!

So all this worrying was over nothing. I was just as abundant, but actually doing something I loved and was passionate about each day. Well, when I realised this and saw how abundant I really am you can guess what happened next...even more money flowed to me! So get real with your finances, it's not bad to know exactly how much you're earning. It gives you a budget to work with where you can feel abundant and you never know you could get a great surprise like I did! When we know exactly how much we have we can be grateful, and that's what shifts your money blocks!

Your relationship with money is really important. It's key to really sit down and have an honest conversation with yourself about your beliefs around money and having it. Some people can be scared of having money out of the fear that their life would change, people would judge them, or they could lose people. Yes, your life would change if you allowed the money to change you. Real, honest friends and family would never judge you for having money. They would support you and celebrate with you. If you believe money would change your life, it's because you believe it would change you. So really get comfortable with this and visualise yourself with your dream house, your dream car, your dream holidays and equally visualise how your money could help people, how you could give back to your community and enhance other people's lives. When you come from a place of love and not ego, you won't change - the money won't define you it will simply be an added extra to your already wealthy life.

Tribe Queen

Finding my tribe was really important to me. I'd always see the quote 'your vibe attracts your tribe' and longed for my spiritual gang. When I first spiritually awoke back in 2016, I was surrounded by negativity. The friends I had were negative, and just weren't my type of people. I clung on to them in fear of being alone, out of fear of not being loved. After splitting up with my ex-boyfriend they were my only form of contact and support. My parents at the time didn't really listen to me or help, so my friends have always been my go to for support.

Now I'm all for giving credit and during these painful times they did listen to me, they saw me and tried to help as best as they could. After a few weeks though and when I started to discover the Law of Attraction, something shifted and all of a sudden they didn't want to talk to me, they didn't want to see me and especially when I'd try to explain white butterflies were stalking me...yeah it got a bit awkward. The truth was, this was not my tribe, and the Universe was simply clearing these people out of my life as I was raising my vibration. I remember so clearly the day I had a suspected mini stroke. Yes, at twenty-three they couldn't explain what happened to me. I had all the symptoms of a mini stroke, and it was shit scary. I was in my flat alone at the time, under huge amounts of stress, worry and pain. When I say I hit rock bottom I really did. I was so lucky to get to the door to open it, call the ambulance and message my friend to call my Dad all before passing out. It was no surprise my body acted out in this way, the paramedics when they arrived were worried but after numerous tests they couldn't find anything wrong with me. Yes, after ALL the symptoms of a stroke they said I had perfect health and everything seemed normal. They couldn't explain what had just happened to me.

I was on bed rest for a few days and told to really watch my stress levels. This is when I knew something had to change. I told my friends what had happened and none of them even believed me! They thought I was lying and didn't even offer to come and see me. This is when I knew things had to change. I walked away from the first set of friends as peacefully as I could. My best friend at the time then revealed to me by accident that she had been sabotaging me by messaging my ex-boyfriend and telling him I'd been sleeping with some other guy! I mean it all got absolutely ridiculous, like a scene out of a terrible movie. In the space of a few months I'd lost everyone I held dear to me in my life apart from my family. The Universe was revealing the truth to me; as I was raising my vibration I just wasn't matching these people anymore. They certainly didn't leave without a fight as I explained in my previous chapters, the police were involved, and my Dad was even verbally attacked in public. It's really sad that after all they did they couldn't just leave peacefully.

It took a lot of strength and courage to forgive these actions and to move on, I felt isolated and alone. I was becoming a better person and manifesting so many incredible things into my life, where was my support? A lot of friends came into my life and left, some peacefully, others not. It was heartbreaking that every time I trusted someone and let them in, I'd learn further and be back by myself again. I know now looking back that these people were simply lessons and I needed to meet them and experience them to grow. They were all just characters in my story. We agreed before we came here that they would do this to awaken me and I'm glad they did. It taught me what I wanted from my tribe, and how much love, happiness and abundance I truly deserved.

From these experiences I was determined to attract not only my dream man, but my tribe also. A tribe who were my biggest cheerleaders, asked nothing of me and truly loved my authentic self. Selina was the first person to walk in to my life. I honestly can't begin to tell you what an Angel this woman is. Without Selina I don't think I would have got through this as gracefully as I have. Selina brought The Secret into my life, and together we re-kindled a friendship over spirituality. At the time she was living with her boyfriend a few hours away from me, so although I had her support online as I did with many of my other friends, nothing compares to that human contact in person. I don't know what got me through the days, weeks or months - faith I guess and a knowing that no matter what, I was moving towards an incredible future. I did write a dream best friend list and learnt to become that list just like I became my dream man list. I became love, radiated love and became grateful for all the support I did have from my online friends.

Eventually Selina moved back home to where I live with her boyfriend, and my beautiful goddaughter Isabella was born. Becoming a godmother made all the pain worth it. In that moment nothing else mattered but my unconditional love for this little Angel. An Angel I'd seen so many times stood next to my own daughter in meditation. That was my faith, my belief and the start of my tribe. Throughout this journey I feel like this little family got me through so much. I am eternally grateful for the Universe sending Selina into my life and I know this lady is here to stay.

My best friend Annie is another of my tribe, although I knew her before I awakened, we had drifted apart and didn't see each other much. During the break-up she was incredible but I couldn't ask too much of her as she had just been diagnosed with breast cancer and I didn't want to put her in a position to support me while she was ill. She had my back though and I will never be able to thank her and her fiancé for all their love and support over the years. Especially picking me up at 1am on New Year's Day a crying wreck. These guys are my tribe and deserve a world of happiness.

Lastly Hannah & Natalia, they came into my life last of all through this writing journey. We instantly connected and I feel like I've known them both over many lives. The wisdom, love and peace these incredible ladies have brought to my life has been unreal. I am so humbled and grateful to have all these incredible ladies in my life from all walks of life and how we uplift, honour and support one another unconditionally. This didn't happen overnight though and I had to learn exactly what I didn't want in a friendship before I could manifest these earth Angels.

'A real friend is...one who walks in when the rest of the world walks out' - Unknown

This doesn't mean to say that all your friends will filter out of your life now that you're spiritual. Annie didn't. In fact, we grew closer and now she actively practises the Law of Attraction and positivity. Not everyone in your life will get it, but it's the support you want. If they're uplifting you, supporting you and helping you thrive...hold on to these people. If they're not let them go. I did this with my past friends by removing them off social media and doing energy chord cutting exercises. It was tough as some energy vampires will cling on to you for dear life. You may think it's dramatic removing people off social media or blocking them, but to the Universe it's clear. Remember raising your standards is really beneficial to you. Get clear about what you will or won't tolerate in your relationships. Set those free who no longer serve you and simply send them love. The people who are meant to be in your life will never leave and the people who aren't always will.

When you find your tribe, they will more than likely be spiritual or positive like yourself. When I meet with my tribe either all together or by ourselves, I ALWAYS feel uplifted. No matter what fear, doubt or limiting belief I have, I take it to them knowing they will channel the exact advice I need to hear. Surrounding yourself with your spiritual sisters is the best feeling in the world, having a tribe full of women supporting, uplifting and growing together is a powerful force here in the Universe. I now know why none of my other friendships worked out. None of them had this level of knowing, love or divine light. Our conversations now are healing, enriching and together we create a movement of positive energy. This is the kind of ride or die love you need in your life. That unconditional sisterhood love that doesn't dampen a woman's vision, power or spirit but allows her to rise and be able to open up in a safe environment and be authentically raw. It's about creating an environment with no judgement, no fear, only love of yourself, your sister and the divine. I may not have siblings myself, but these ladies are my sisters and my biggest inspirations. Together we face similar struggles, whether that's ego, fear or not believing in the process. No matter what the situation is, we all seem to have the same underlying issue at the same time, meaning that we work together to heal.

You should never have to settle for company because it feels safe. Sometimes even in company we can feel completely alone. Attracting your tribe is all about matching the vibration, so becoming YOUR best friend first. Love yourself, heal yourself and be your biggest cheerleader and that's exactly how you will attract your soul sisters into your life. It's funny I've never had any issues, disagreements or arguments with ANY of my tribe and I've known some of them ten years now. That's the key with your tribe, when you're in alignment and totally supported there is nothing to argue about or drama. There is only love for one another.

So right now, if you're in the position I was in, have faith. Know your worth, and that you don't need to settle for friends. You're an incredible person with a lot of love to give to this world and you should never have to settle for anything less than amazing. Anything is possible, so get yourself out there. If you want to meet more like-minded people, go to a yoga class, meditation class, a spiritual church. Whatever you feel drawn to, take up a new hobby. If that's not possible then join some online communities. I myself have a Law of Attraction support group on Facebook, which you're all of course welcome to join. Groups like this are incredible. Not only is it a safe place to post and feel supported, but you also get talking to people and can make friends. I did this a lot in the beginning. I would join Law of Attraction groups on Facebook and talk to people. A lot of the groups were quite negative and there was a lot of desperation, so I would only message people I vibed with and it felt good. I met some really incredible ladies who I still speak to now and these were my tribe at that time in my life. I could turn to them when I needed support or reassurance. The beautiful thing I found was that we were all kind of going through the same thing at that time and I totally believe we were all meant to connect. The Universe has a beautiful way of bringing people together so whether that's online or in person, when you set the intentions and take inspired action it will happen.

For those who are asking how can we improve current friendships, ask yourself, do they add value to my life? Do they uplift, inspire and fulfil me? If the answer is yes, then you can do many things. Speaking positively about that person and situation is one. Our thoughts and words are constant manifestations so make sure you're speaking what you want to happen in your reality. If you want to work on forgiveness, then you can make a list of all the wonderful things that person has done for you throughout your friendship and lessons you've learnt through their actions. Also reflect what you'd like to manifest, so treat that person exactly how you'd like to be treated. Like attracts like. If that still doesn't work and you're feeling drained, or just not on the same level, then it's important you walk away and let the Universe do its job. If I hadn't of been brave enough to walk away from numerous people over the last few years, then I wouldn't have the incredible sisters I have in my life today. The Universe will never leave you at a loss, sometimes people leave so another bigger and brighter door opens for us to step through.

One thing I've certainly learnt with my tribe over the last year, is that speaking our truth must come from within us. There are times where I've seen my spiritual sisters be mistreated and it would be so easy for me to jump into ego and tell them what I think they should do. There are times where my sisters have also told me their opinions and judgements. We all do it we're human. We want to protect our friends and ensure they're safety. One beautiful thing we've learnt as a group is that we can't vibe for one another, and we need to leave our ego's and judgements at the door. When one of us needs the others we should be loving and returning them to love not passing judgements on their decisions or life choices. This was a powerful revelation for us, as there were times I thought I should voice my opinion but I'm glad I didn't because I was wrong. I'm glad I was wrong and that my friend worked out the best path for herself, this is the key as spiritual sisters we should simply help one another along our paths not try to force our truth onto them. Only we as individuals know our truth, only we can vibe what feels real and honest to us no one else. All we can do is support and be love and that is all that is required from a sisterhood. We need to let them make their own choices as they know best. Trust that your friend has this, because darling she does! It may not look like it, but she has a plan, the Universe has a plan for her and your job is to be her biggest cheerleader no matter what. Remind her to return to love, and go within for answers and most importantly leave your ego at the door. It won't serve her nor will it serve your highest good passing judgements on her life. Only we know our truth, and our truth may be different to your friends, they all learn in time and I'm glad I was wrong, because it showed that was purely my ego passing judgement rather than allowing her to make her own destiny. Sometimes we should speak up yes, if we can see our sister in pain we should use our voice. We should try to help, but make sure that comes from the most sincere place and isn't in the heat of the moment.

At the end of the day, we will never truly feel what someone else does within, so we have to trust that they are making the best decisions for themselves at any given time. It's healthy to have these conversations with your spiritual tribe, and that's the beauty of them they will get your concerns and bringing up any funky feelings allows them to heal. Your true tribe will respond positively and lovingly so don't be afraid to ask for support, or ask them to release judgement we're all human and are constantly learning. As a sisterhood you learn and you rise together.

I've met such beautiful souls through my work also. Being self-employed does have an impact of how many new people you can meet daily, especially if you work from home. It suits me though, and I of course talk to so many of you online.

Working with brands, press and especially spiritual press really helps me as I meet so many lovely genuine people along the way. I've always found anybody who works in spirituality is going to be a good egg. I always feel recharged when dealing with them, and it just makes my working life so much easier and way more fulfilling. Especially in the media industry. It's so refreshing to work with people who actually want to share your story with the world exactly how you've written it. No fabrications, exaggerations, or lies. They have your best interests at heart, and value your work. This is how I've also made great friends from inviting them on my podcast, meeting them at spiritual events I speak at and even being featured on their platforms. There are a million ways to meet spiritual or like-minded friends, so stop stressing about the how's and enjoy the process. Get out there, have fun, be your own best friend, and remember joy is the ultimate creator.

"You were not created to walk your path alone. Your circle does not have to be plentiful, it just needs to elevate you higher."

—Minaa B

Self-Love Queen

I felt that self-love deserved its own chapter. We so often overlook the need to work on our self-love when in fact, 99.9% of the time the answer to all of our worries comes back to self-love. We live in a world where people are selfish and do take us light workers for granted, but there is also a large majority of incredible souls out there who also understand this. With celebrities, influencers and TV shows now dictating the way we should look, act and speak - it's no wonder we live in a world where we struggle to love ourselves. It feels wrong, weird or even egotistical to say that we love ourselves but hun this is all old programming, it is perfectly safe to love and respect yourself.

Before I was spiritual, I really didn't love myself at all. I'd battled body dysmorphia since my teenage years and had gone on crazy diets in order to achieve my perfect body. The things I'd put my poor body through to look 'perfect' was ridiculous and do you know what, my body never ever gave up on me, it loved me that much - remember that your body has never given up on you! As I grew into my adult years no matter what weight I was, I was miserable. I hated the way the way I looked, and nothing would fill that void. I kept thinking a guy could fill this massive void in my soul, but the honest truth was no one could fill it but me. I had no respect for myself either, I let my boyfriends' influence me and they even made me hate myself even more through making me feel uncomfortable about my body. I was a hot mess of unworthiness, but this was ALL simply in my head. An illusion I was telling myself over and over for years.

Even when I became spiritual I really struggled to see myself as worthy and deserving of love and my desires. I really had to dig deep and make the year I was single a self-love mission. After years of old programming and negative thinking, it was not going to be an easy journey. Even when I made breakthroughs and stood up for myself the Universe would soon test me to see if I was learning. Being a Virgo I'm a natural giver, I like to help people and if I can I'll fix it. The problem is, although I meant well I was taking the power away from the person to heal themselves. They needed to learn how to float themselves through love.

As the saying goes you can't love anyone unless you love yourself and this is very true. We are all holding up big mirrors to one another and reflecting the love we feel for ourselves. Just as bullies do, they don't pick on you because you are unworthy, they pick on you because they are projecting their own lack and insecurities onto someone who is confident and carefree. If a lover isn't giving you the love and care you need it's not because you're not worthy of their love it's because they feel they aren't worthy of your love or their own. I'd also invite you to see that the love you're craving from them can also be given to you through working on yourself and filling your own cup. It's so important that we continuously work on our own self-love and peace within so that our outer experiences and relationships can reflect this too.

When we choose to love ourselves, we invite into our lives so much abundance and positive experiences. I am so proud that I dedicated a year to loving myself instead of desperately seeking the dream man and becoming a man eater. I knew this was the first time in my life that I had an excuse to love myself, I wanted my husband to love me and accept me so first of all I had to give that to myself. I wanted to be able to give him my highest level of love and respect also, and I could only do that once I truly loved and accepted myself. So, if you're looking to manifest your dream partner, it's got to be an inside job first. When I first became single I hated being lonely, I hated sitting at home in my own company because it felt weird. After some time and having to accept that this was my reality, I embraced my own company, I surrendered to it and worked on my self-love.

The reason why I hated being by myself was because I was fearing myself, I was fearing addressing all the negativity from my past and my past wounds. But you see, when I addressed them, healed them and accepted myself fully my whole world changed. I started to love my own company, I enjoyed it and I wanted to take time out of my week for some me time. I still do this now and think it's vital that we learn to be comfortable in our company and with our thoughts. When you're hoping to attract love, you have to become that love, you need to radiate love from within which means working on your self-love. So instead of throwing yourself on the dating scene commit to yourself first, commit to your own self-development and get real about what you want in your dream partner. Remember the Universe is one big mirror to us, so if we don't fully love and accept ourselves, every inch of ourselves, then we are not on the vibration of love that will attract that forever love. Choosing to be single, or even choosing to be exclusive to yourself isn't weird or pushing away that dream love, it's an act of self-love and respect for your own needs.

The same works for weight loss. I've battled with my weight for years with yo-yo dieting and my weight ranging between a size 8-16. I've never stayed the same weight consistently. This was reflective of my situations at the time and depression. Now that I'm spiritual I've remained the same size through finding peace with my body and self-love. Even when I found the Law of Attraction I didn't lose weight immediately, it was only when I let the dream body go and fully learnt to embrace and love every part of me right now that it dropped off in a matter of weeks. So now, every time I think I could do with toning up, I don't freak out about it, I learn how to love the part of me that I feel needs changing and it changes when I realise I don't need to change anything about me because I'm already so beautiful and so loved as I am.

The most important relationship in this life, is the one we have with ourselves. At the end of the day, relationships come and go, family come and go, everything can come and go in an instance but the only consistent and loyal person in our life is us. Yet, we're so quick to insult ourselves and even sometimes hate ourselves. Before you look outside yourself for that happiness, that marriage, that happily ever after, that job, that house, that whatever, the answer will always come back to loving yourself before anything else. You can't fill anyone else's cup if you can't even fill your own, and plot twist you don't need to fill anyone else's cup either, that's their responsibility not ours.

It's all about connecting with your heart, instead of your head. Your head is a great tool for logistical thinking but follow and centre yourself in your heart it's safe to do this and it will never lead you astray. From today commit to loving yourself more, be kinder and more gentle. Cry when you want to, eat what you want and be your biggest freakin' cheerleader. When you work with yourself instead of fighting against yourself - it's the best relationship in the world.

Being kind to yourself is so important in the journey of self-love. We so often give our power away to other people and neglect our own needs and cup filling to help and please others. It's time you reclaimed your power, take back your control, take back your energy and wrap yourself up in one big Spiritual Queen vibin' hug! This is your time and your life, you decide how you feel and who you should give your precious energy to. Sometimes saying no is the biggest act of self-love, saying no to plans, to friends, to lovers, to family. Saying no isn't being cruel or negative, it's being kind to you. If you don't want to do something honour that, there's a reason why you're feeling this way. Sometimes an evening spent in alone in a hot bath reading a great book is all we need to say yes to ourselves for once. That's what this entire book is about, saying YASS to you! No one else. You're born into this world just you, and you'll transition from this world just you. I know this can be a scary concept, but when you become your own best friend and love yourself, you connect to your truth and you realise that we are all connected, there is no separation, and we don't die, we can never die, our souls are eternal. All that happens is we transition back to the spirit realm ready to be reunited with our soul family, guides and Angels to have one big epic celebration together (or so I'd like to think, just putting that out there for my soul family because we will be having one big celebration).

There were days when I couldn't write this book, when I couldn't show up spiritually, they were few, but I had them. It was when I needed to in fact work on myself, I needed to heal past wounds and receive miracles myself in my own personal life. I did feel like a failure some days, but then I realised I'm still doing the work either way. Whether it's showing up to my spiritual business and creating content or showing up for myself, I was always showing up to learn, grow and become peaceful. The key to self-love is to flow, like I mentioned previously honour your feelings and truth every single day. Even if that's dedicating a day to you, to pamper yourself, nourish your soul and binge on self-help videos, babe, you're still doing the work in a magnificent way.

I myself dedicate time each week to do some self-love practises. These are so important because just like Law of Attraction and gratitude practises you can't just do them once and your sorted for life. Repetition is key and will allow you to stay constantly in a state of love and harmony with yourself. The first practise I recommend is Louise Hay's 'Mirror Work' - I love this practise because it's something so simple that we can do it every day and it doesn't take much time at all. Mirror Work is essentially what it says on the tin, work you do in the mirror. I personally love doing this in the morning to set me up for the day ahead, but there are no right or wrong answers here, do what feels best for you as that's an act of self-love in itself! In this Mirror Work I will tell myself 'Emma I really, really love you', now this may seem vain, egotistical and believe me your ego will scream at you the first few times you do this as it will seem so out of the ordinary. Really look into your eyes and feel the love, they say it takes 21 days to change a habit so stick to this for at least 21 days straight. You will notice big and happy changes in your self-love and how you feel in general. I also have conversations with myself during *Mirror Work*, if I need a pep talk, some motivation or need to be my own shoulder to cry on, I'm there saying exactly what I need to hear in the mirror and being my biggest fan. This is the beauty with *Mirror Work*, it's such a personal practise and by looking at yourself in the mirror, you make this personal and you can own your truth in that moment.

Another practise I like to do is called a self-love list, in which I will write down all the points I love about myself and fill up a whole A4 page. Don't worry if you can't do that to start off with, note down as many as you can, quantity isn't important it's all about the quality of each point! Get really specific and celebrate all the amazing things you love about yourself. This can be your strength, your patience, your kind hearted nature, your killer bum, your beautiful hair, whatever way feels right to you, get listing those points. Once you've finished your list, I want you to go and read each point out loud in the mirror and look into your eyes as you're repeating them. At the end you should feel pretty yummy and connected to your heart, just thank yourself, really thank yourself for doing this practise and for being there for one another through everything. Once you've finished your *Mirror Work* with this self-love list, I want you to do something peculiar, place this list underneath your bed with a piece of Rose Quartz on top. The amount of time you leave it under the bed doesn't matter, it could be a day, a week or forever it's up to you! I personally like to keep mine under there, then pull it out whenever I need a pick me up. I don't know how this practise works but it bloody does! I always feel so loved and looked after when I do this and have recommended this practise to so many of my coaching clients and they too feel huge positive changes after doing this practise.

Another practise I do regularly to help increase my self-love is treating myself. Whether it be a bunch of flowers, some clothes or a holiday, I treat myself often to show that I'm worthy and deserving of all the abundance the Universe has to offer. Treating yourself means that you see yourself as worthy of your hard efforts, that you're worthy of your time and effort. If that means a spa day with your besties, or a romantic trip away with your partner, whatever brings you joy - do it! The more fun you're having, the more joy you create in your life, the Universe responds to this in amazing ways. Joy is the ultimate creator, so when you're fully accepting yourself, loving life and most importantly loving YOU the Universe has no option but to bring so much more joy and abundance into your life.

Most self-love issues can be related back to the heart chakra also. This chakra is mighty and for me is the one chakra that continuously needs opening and cleansing. No matter how many times I do meditation, it's an on-going practise

to re-align and centre myself back into that heart space.
I simply do a heart chakra mediation on YouTube that
breathes green heart energy into your heart chakra and
helps to release anything blocking you from being fully
open and present. Mixed with chants and visualisations
this meditation really helps me to feel the love again and be
aligned in the present.

I would recommend to do these self-love practises each
week, it's so important you maintain these acts of self-love
in whatever way feels good for you. You may create your
own rituals and practises, even just soaking in the bath and
taking some 'me' time to re-align is self-love. The key to
this is intention and being present for yourself.

Inner child work can really aid you in your self-love
journey also. Our inner child needs nurturing just as we do.
Sometimes a lot of our blocks to love can be held in our
inner child. Simple meditations can help you to speak with
your inner child and address any fears they may have. You
can imagine during meditation your inner child in front
of you, at any age it doesn't matter let it naturally come to
you, and give them a big hug. Ask them what do they need
to hear today? What is troubling them? You can then reply
giving them some loving and encouraging words to reassure
them just like you would with your own child. Once you've
done this imagine putting those fears with your inner child
in a box in front of you and imagine blowing it up together.
Simple practises like this can really help to heal your inner
child and insure their happiness is met which will in return
allow you to feel more at peace with your own love.

Self-love is a powerful thing and if you can dedicate time each day or week to these practises and your own, you will notice how calm, peaceful and loving your life will become. You'll notice your blocks fade away and abundance will pour into your life. The more you love yourself and continue with this, even your outer relationships in your life will transform and be full of the same respectful, loyal and genuine love.

"To love yourself right now, just as you are, is to give yourself heaven. Don't wait until you die. If you wait, you die now. If you love, you live now."

—Alan Cohen

Powerful Queen

Now you may think this is weird title for a chapter but let me explain to you the power of my cheese paradox. Many years ago, back when I was around sixteen, I remember living at my parents' house and had turned on the TV. There was a farming programme on in which they were explaining the benefits of cheese. Now as a cheese lover this certainly grabbed my attention. Now excuse my way of explaining this as I am certainly no medical professional or nutritionist. They were explaining that when cheese moves through your intestines that it drags all the crap and fat sat in there, so effectively it helps clear you out and helps with weight loss. Now as an impressionable teen who wanted to lose weight, this cheese revelation was the answer to all my muffin top prayers!

I followed this advice and low and behold the more I ate cheese I would lose weight especially around my stomach. I've carried this groundbreaking medical weight loss secret for years and just presumed everyone knew that cheese helped you lose weight. Up until very recently I've sworn by this and because I love cheese it's just been a win win situation. It was only when discussing my love for cheese with my spiritual sisters that my perfect cheesy world was about to be rocked. My sisters were telling me that actually cheese holds a lot of fat and that it doesn't make you lose weight at all! After some googling I found that my cheese paradox was completely false - but how was I different? How was I losing the weight every time I ate cheese? Well my love's, welcome to the power of your thoughts!

I felt like this topic deserved its own chapter away from Law of Attraction basics, because although it is a basic step in Law of Attraction, the further we go into spirituality we seem to forget the essentials. The lesson for the power of my thoughts first came from when I was flying to the Maldives with my love. I've always been an anxious flyer and any turbulence sends my heart racing as I hate the feeling in my stomach. Normally I always say before flying 'Thank you Universe for a safe, calm and happy flight'. This time I was going to need more. Every time I felt turbulence which just felt endless I would say to myself 'I am safe, I am well, I am calm'. I must have said this for an hour straight over and over in my head to try and not focus on the crippling fear I felt. Every time I kept saying this mantra the turbulence would stop. After a traumatic flight there, on the flight back I was determined to own the power of my thoughts. Before the flight I said 'Thank you Universe for a smooth, turbulent free, calm flight'. Even when little moments of turbulence happened I would say 'Thank you Universe for a turbulent free flight. I am safe, I am calm, I am well'. I kid you not, every time I did this and imagined Angels holding the wings of the plane the turbulence would stop. Now you think this would have been enough to make me think 'Damn Emma you've got some skills here!' No.

The next example came like I said when I was sat with my spiritual sisters over dinner talking about my revolutionary cheese diet. We laughed about how for years I had literally trained my mind to believe that when I eat cheese it's clearing out my gut and helping me to lose weight. I had created my own diet with the power of my thoughts. I believed it whole heartedly because I'd seen it on TV - obviously now I'm awakened I realise we shouldn't always believe what we see on TV. I just found it hilarious that once again with the power of my thoughts I had spoken this weight loss method entirely into existence.

Now the reason why the cheese paradox worked for me was because on this TV show they showed a diagram of how cheese clears out your insides. I had no reason to doubt this and therefore took it as fact. Now I know you may be thinking 'Oh great so I'll train my mind to think every time I eat chocolate I'm losing weight!' I'm not saying that's impossible, it's not, but you wouldn't believe it. I'm sure after months of repeating these affirmations and believing in your weight loss, it would eventually happen as you would have trained your mind to believe, but the key to Law of Attraction is your trust and belief. I had no doubt whatsoever in my cheese diet, so the Universe had no choice but to allow this thought to manifest because I believed wholeheartedly. The same goes for the stories we tell ourselves, just like thoughts our words are an even more powerful creator.

The lesson came from my love. I talk more about this in the next few chapters about facing my ego, and my darkest fears. As amazing as our relationship had been for many months, some challenging issues started to come up (hello twin flames) and this is what triggered me to look into twin flames more closely. After our break, which I explain in the next chapter, things still weren't all sunshine and roses. I couldn't understand it. I thought about how far I'd come and how much I'd spiritually awoken even further, and things still weren't better. I was reading *A Course In Miracles* and suddenly it hit me like a truck, we become the stories we tell ourselves. Thoughts manifest, we speak into existence constantly and what had I been doing for the last six months...yeah you guessed it, complaining and being a victim about everything he was doing. So guess what I was manifesting...yup more shit! This really opened my eyes because it was so true, and how could I have not seen this. I wasn't accepting him for who he was, I wasn't even accepting myself. Every time he'd do something crappy I'd tell my friends, talk about it with several other friends, repeat it in my head and think 'Damn what a dick'. He wasn't though. This was the story I was telling myself. So guess what happened, more and more things started manifesting until we got to a pretty shit place. Neither of us knew why this was happening or why we couldn't just get back to how we were before. Little did I know I held the key to this little gem. No matter how many times it was probably right in front of me, it took the Universe separating us again for me to finally see the self-sabotage I had created in our lives.

> **'Life will keep bringing you the same test
> over and over again until you learn your
> lesson' - Unknown**

When I realised the power of my thoughts and especially words, I knew I had to change immediately. So instead of focusing on lack, hurt, or the separation, I remembered that separation is simply a human concept and doesn't actually exist. I wrote a new story, literally. In my journal, I wrote our truth. I wrote a whole A4 page on our truth, and how we were together, happy and totally accepting of one another. I wrote all the happy things we do together and chose this story. I removed the illusion, the past was in the past, and only happiness and love existed now. I told my spiritual sisters my plan and that from now on I would never complain again, never speak of lack, only our amazing abundant loving relationship to everyone who asked. I also wrote a list of affirmations to read out daily about us, how we accept one another, feel comfortable in our twin flame union and how loving we were to one another and happy. I know before if I had done this I wouldn't have felt good reading them, but now I realised that I had manifested this shit storm I knew how to get us out. I renamed his phone contact to 'LOVE ONLY ♥' and made the pact with myself that I would only reply to the truth. If he replied anything negative, I would send him love through my thoughts, and not reply. I was ONLY putting energy into truth and love. I made sure the Universe knew that and once again only thought of all our happiness and love.

When I read the affirmations each day and thought positive thoughts about us it honestly did comfort me, it felt like the cloak of illusion had finally been lifted off and I could be free to love him unconditionally again.

A big shift had happened, I could feel it and I could feel it in him although we weren't together in the psychical. I was reminded constantly through signs of his presence, his love and the power of my thoughts. I started seeing white butterflies everywhere again, I was watching the final ever episode of my beloved *Once Upon A Time* and the famous quote came up that always finds me and reminds me of my love 'I will always find you, always'. It's funny as I have 'always' tattooed on my arm, and got it engraved on his watch I gave him with our anniversary date on also. I connected so strongly to him during meditation and was reassured by all who appeared to me including my love that everything was okay and finally the truth could be seen. It was like a weight had been lifted from me, finally I realised why we had battled this for so long. I was battling this with my thoughts and with my words, I had talked my worst fears into existence.

I know many of you will be asking how I could be so sure, keep the faith during this time and simply...believe. It was like I had been prepared for this, I felt like the Universe had sent me clues years before of how to deal with this. When I turned my whole existence into a positive experience with him and re-wrote our story the Universe had no option but to make that my reality. Now it's important for me to state here that sometimes, no matter how hard we try, things may not manifest for a number of reasons, divine timing or it's simply just not meant to be. I felt that false belief with my ex when I tried to manifest him back. I always had a sinking feeling in my gut and could never get to a state of truly believing because my intuition was telling me otherwise. This time it was different, I knew it in my soul, I knew it in my heart that we would be reunited and that what lay ahead of us was going to be epic. So I was able to relax, be present and just love him, love myself and be love. I was having fun, something I hadn't done in a long time under this illusion. I was so certain of the outcome, and we were already together, happy and in love. As soon as I started speaking into existence and feeling the love for him the whole game changed.

It's so important to be aware of your thoughts and your words. Are you someone like I used to be who would discuss negative situations and dwell in lack? I totally get that it's healthy to want to get this frustration out and receive guidance from others, that's healthy. What's not doing you any favours is the way in which you portray these stories. I would get so absorbed, and really talk negatively about my love and the relationship. So ONLY speak what you'd want to bring into existence. Start rewriting your story today and choose again. Always choose love. We can alter any situation in our lives as hopeless as they may seem at the time. Write your affirmations, say them in the mirror each day until you do believe them. Only speak positively of people, situations and yourself. Leave the past in the past and speak as if it has already miraculously got better. You'll be surprised at how quickly you feel a million times better and the situation magically improves. It's key to always work on forgiveness during this time. Are you holding onto resentment, anger or pain? Let that shit go and remember you are the author of your life.

I do also want to point out that I have tried this with friends during my life, and the situation didn't improve and that was only because I knew I had to walk away and it wasn't meant to be. Try all of the above, send them love, but if you feel you need to walk away then you already know the answer. You can always ask your guides, Angels or simply the Universe for guidance on what you should do.

I want to remind you that no matter what stage you're at in your spiritual journey, we all continue to learn and grow. No matter how basic this logic may seem, and how much in the beginning we are taught this in Law of Attraction - we all forget it at some stage. This needed to happen to awaken us further and for me to be able to write this chapter. I think over any basic, the power of our thoughts and words has to be the most vital for me as it effects so much of what we manifest into our reality. If I could speak cheese into being a weight loss tool, stop a plane's turbulence and hurt my relationship in the past with words, anything is possible. So now is the time to really watch what you say and remember before you speak, think - would I like this to happen in real life?

There are many quotes I could use right now to remind you of the power of your thoughts and words, but this one specifically from *A Course In Miracles* shifted my existence so I hope it has the same awakening power on you.

"There is no world apart from what you wish, and herein lies your ultimate release. Change but your mind on what you want to see, and all the world must change accordingly"

—A Course In Miracles

Letting Go Queen

"I just want to be on my own" were the crushing words that my dream man told me a year into our relationship. Things had been rocky for a few months and that initial magical feeling had somehow got very lost. For months I had fought myself, him and resisted overtime the Universe had guided me to awaken further. I had been resisting the most vital part of the Law of Attraction, letting go. It's odd I always had in my mind that I wanted to include a chapter all about letting go and spiritually surrendering - yet here I was a newbie to the whole concept. So how could I have manifested so powerfully in the last two years but be faced with losing my dream man altogether. The answer is - I had to learn something first. That lesson was to spiritually surrender and let go of all control of my life.

Hi my name's Emma and I used to be an absolute controlling nightmare. I thought at first it was just the Virgo in me but being faced with my worst nightmare of losing my dream man I realised...shit I've been a nightmare. I'd read so much about surrendering the outcome during my studies of the Law of Attraction but somehow never practised it. So in true Universe style it pulled the carpet from underneath me and said 'How are you going to control your life now, Emma?' At first I fell straight into the blame game and thought well it's him who has to do the work, it's nothing to do with me. The more I was forced to spend time by myself I realised that actually over the last five months I've really been neglecting my self-love and I just wasn't me. My ego and fear had slowly but surely crept into my mind and our relationship. It was also uncanny that we went on a break the same week I'd split up with my ex two years prior. That was the first synchronicity, it just got freaky after that.

It then dawned upon me that maybe this was the test, to see whether I'd learnt from last time and would surrender my happily ever after I'd wanted so badly. I really went within and focused on what I did last time round and did the complete opposite. It was weird when I first met my twin flame. I always said that we would go on a two week break which would do us the world of good and here I was living that prophecy. Although I was scared, fearful and living out my biggest fears of abandonment and losing him, I felt this odd kind of certainty that it would all be okay. I was sat in my office at my desk a few days into the break distracting myself with work. I have a small book collection on my desk of books I'd bought but haven't read. I felt drawn to Gabrielle Bernstein's - 'The Universe Has Your Back'. I don't know why but I picked it up and flicked to what I thought was a random page. The chapter read 'When You Think You've Surrendered Surrender More'…boom exactly what I needed to see. I had seen the words surrender quite a few times and honestly thought I was chilled about the outcome. The truth was I was chilled but inside I hadn't spiritually surrendered all my plans to God.

Before our break I won't lie I had every month for the next three years planned out. Even the month we'd get engaged, buy a house, get married and get pregnant. Crazy I know, seeing as most of these were totally out of my control anyway! I don't know how I'd got here and why I was turning my whole life into one big checklist. I really analysed my thoughts and realised I was trying to control everything out of fear, not out of love. I was so scared to lose him that guess what I manifested...losing him! Once I'd realised what a control freak I'd been and how much I could actually laugh at myself for all of this, I turned to Gabby's book and read the entire book that day. It was what I needed, every single word of it.

My love wasn't talking to me at this point. I actually had no hope presented to me in the physical. All I had was my intuition and the Universe guiding me. We had our dream holiday booked to the Maldives for a month's time. How could something so perfect have gone so downhill. I spent the first week spiritually surrendering through Gabby's book and really worked on my feelings towards marriage, kids and houses. I realised that I wanted them for all the wrong reasons, fear instead of love. After reading Gabby talk about the book 'A Course In Miracles', I knew instantly this is what I wanted teach to people through my work. I also signed up for an online Reiki course as for the first time in my life I felt drawn to the concept. It's funny my psychic Rachel had told me for years I was going to have healing hands and I'd always laugh it off thinking Reiki sounded too out there for me. It was my time though, I had awoken once again and was ready to step further into my spirituality.

A week had gone past now and still I felt like I'd made no progress, I'd had minimal contact with him and truthfully to an outsider I'm sure they would have said 'Love he's not coming back'. I worried about being so vocal online about our relationship as I suddenly thought 'What if I'm left embarrassed and humiliated if he doesn't come back?' I knew in that moment I had to trust my gut and nothing else. I saw my three spirit guides or my boyband as I like to call them. They showed us in the Maldives laughing and having a good time, something which seemed so impossible at that time. They said it was all meant to happen like this and to surrender everything I thought I needed. This was it, just as Gabby's book had also taught me. The Universe had an incredible plan ahead for me but I was stepping in and controlling everything. I began to realise everything I'd manifested was great but it actually really didn't fulfil me in life. I was happy but not fulfilled. Maybe the Universe did know better...it did know better! I only had to look at the situation with my ex-boyfriend to realise that if I had manifested him back successfully, I wouldn't have all the happiness I have now with my dream man. At that moment I knew I had to let go of every outcome, timing or ring I had in mind. The Universe knew better and I had to get out of its way.

From that moment on I relaxed. I took my hands off the steering wheel of life and spiritually surrendered to the Universe. So from now on when people ask me what I'm doing in life I just say 'God's got a great plan and when I need to know it will be shown to me'. Wow I genuinely can't believe control freak Mumford is writing that she has let go! A week had gone by and I had found so much peace and solace within myself. Although I had no comfort in our reunion in the psychical I just knew.

The next morning I woke up and said 'He's going to text me today'. I told my spiritual sisters to which they replied 'Let it go!' Just like that I let it go and my phone lit up with a text from him. Instantly I knew I could trust my intuition through this time and once again I was reminded love always wins. I didn't understand why this was happening at the time, but it was essential that during that period, that I go within and learn what I needed to. This kept happening throughout the two week break. I'd be like 'Today I'm going to hear from him' and I did every single time. My spirit guide boyband also kept me feeling supported and loved. They went a bit quiet over the last week but when I asked they said 'He needs us more right now, you know you've done brilliantly so just trust us, you've got this'.

I also channeled this message from my spirit guides during a meditation found in Gabby's book. 'You already know the answer. Let go and the visions will flow. Put your trust in us and we will bring you what you desire. We're working on him and on you, your job is to turn up and expand your mindset. Move through fear and address your old beliefs. You are safe and loved. We have a plan, one which will be revealed really soon. Your daughter sends her love and wants you to know that you are always loved and looked after. The Angels are with you and you're doing a great job at healing. We would never cause you harm, we want you to be happy. You will be a wife and a mother, a great one. We have a plan trust us.'

I knew we'd be back together in every ounce of my being, but I was scared and wanted to spiritually surrender. I was scared what my followers would think, but I realised all of this was ego. The only real thing in this world is love. I had done so well to surrender, surrender some more and let go. I was using Doreen Virtue's *'Angel Answers'* oracle cards each day and all of the cards were so positive and that we'd be back together.

The next blow was my *Soul & Spirit magazine* article coming out about how I manifested my twin flame. I'd manifested this incredible double page article and even made it onto the front cover but I felt like a fraud because right now we weren't together. I couldn't even find one part to be happy about as I missed him so much. The one person who I wanted to show and celebrate with I couldn't. Even the title of my article to my surprise as I didn't have a say was 'Our twin flame is forever' I needed to trust. I surrendered even more. Gabby's book was an absolute godsend through this period as I realised how much my hands were on the steering wheel of my life. I was blocking all of the love and abundance the Universe had planned for me. I did a manifestation/letting go practice from her book where you write down your desire then burn it a week later. Of course, I wanted us to be together, so I wrote it once then surrendered the outcome. When burning it a week later, I'd never seen something burn so fast it in my life and to an absolute crisp. Clearly, I was ready to let it go! I then took a deep breath and let go. Next thing I know I got a text from him, this happened a lot, every time I'd surrender and it was really freaky! Another week passed and I just felt lost. I'd done so much work within myself and 100% surrendered every plan in my life, qualified in Reiki, started *A Course in Miracles* and felt we'd be together, so why wasn't it happening?

I went within and asked my spirit guides. They said 'Don't you get it, you've done the hard part which was to manifest him, how did you have all that belief you'd find an absolute stranger?' They were right I knew this wasn't over and I was sat here worrying about nothing. My Angel cards said exactly the same, and how did I know it would be two weeks? That day I had a really healing conversation with my family which was long overdue. I felt like a weight had been lifted and I felt like I'd past the test and fully surrendered my life. That evening I sat watching 'Sex and The City' movies as they always make me laugh. I realised I watched this when I became single before and thought 'Wow look how far I've come, look how strong I am'. Last time I was an absolute wreck and this time I've become an even better version of myself. When I went to bed that night, I pulled a few Angel cards that read, 'You're ready, perfect timing and you've completed your learning'. I was shocked the Universe was giving me such clear messages. I then had an absolute overwhelming feeling that tomorrow we'd be back together. I was like 'Release and let go Emma, what will be will always be'. I started worrying about why I felt like it would be tomorrow when I hadn't really heard from him in two weeks. I asked my spirit guides and they said 'Emma it's happening tomorrow c'mon get excited!' I thought 'No I need to surrender, how can I trust this?' to which they replied, 'How did you trust that when you got your tattoo you'd meet him the next day?'

The next morning, I called my friend and I had a bit of cry. My newsletter host sends me an email each week of my unsubscribes. Normally I don't read it as I always think the people who need to be subscribed will be, but something that day made me read it and his name was on it. To this day I don't know why I hit the roof about this, at least now I can laugh about the hilarity of the situation. After everything I'd been through him unsubscribing from my newsletter pushed me over the edge…hello ego much!

I was hurt and to me that felt like he was cutting me out of his life for good. My friend reminded me to think what God would say in this situation. The main themes and guidance I was receiving over the last few weeks had been that there is no such thing as twin flame separation and the only separation I had from him was a perception here in my ego. I remember thinking God would laugh at this and say 'Emma up here newsletter's don't even exist so chill babes!' I explained to my friend what I'd felt about him coming back to me today and she said to just keep surrendering, make alternative plans for the Maldives and just keep working on self-love. I couldn't shake this feeling as hard as I tried, we even joked about how one day I'll be telling this story on stage to people and how funny it will be. That evening after a busy work day, I felt myself getting ready. I was like what am I doing?! Yet I still touched up my makeup and re-did my hair. I then went and watched some TV and my doorbell went, I knew 100% it was him. We got back together two weeks exactly to the day after we split, and I just felt such an overwhelming feeling of gratitude and love for him. I realised exactly where I'd been going wrong and how important it is to let go of every expectation I had for my life, the Universe knew better.

The reason I learnt to not manifest so hard anymore is because I don't want control of my life. This whole experience taught me what a bridezilla of life I had become and I didn't even have a ring on my finger yet. I was controlling circumstances and almost holding the Universe at gunpoint to conform to my demands and timeframes. I had to return to love. I felt like the Universe had sent me back to school and awakened me further into divine love and guidance. I'd connected to my spirit guide boyband, became a healer and learnt that the only thing real in this life is love, everything else is all smoke and mirrors of this world. I don't want any more psychic readings as let's face it I think I can be a credible source for myself now anyway. It's not that I don't think they're great, Rachel has provided me with incredibly warming and loving readings. In my opinion I was using them as a timeframe calculator rather than a loving message from my guides. I'm still so shocked the Universe allowed me to know so much in advance, but it was because I was flowing and in alignment with love. I've realised that really all we should be attracting is love and abundance so if that's in the form of lots of money great, if that's in the form of a book deal great - but whatever is meant for me will never miss me. It took being thrown into my biggest fear of being alone to truly heal from all my past wounds.

Another great example of letting go, is this book. I had my heart set on one particular publisher as I just admired all their work so greatly. I pitched to them and was entered into a competition where one person would win a book deal with them. The process was around six months and the night before I just felt so anxious and down about it all after feeling so confident. I realised that over the six months not only had I grown and learnt so much spiritually that I didn't love the chapters anymore, I had also fallen out of love with why I wanted to write this book in the first place.

I was so focused on the validation, money and success it would bring that I forgot the true meaning of being an author. To share love and healing into the world. This book was not to say 'Hey look I made it'. It's to teach, to inspire and most importantly to help you heal. This book was for *you* not me. So the night before I let go of everything and held myself accountable to this act of ego. I pulled an Angel card that read 'There's something better' at that moment I knew I wouldn't win the competition and that the Universe had a great plan for me.

I found peace in realising that I had already won - I had re-branded into Spiritual Queen, started a podcast, spoken at two events and been on the front cover of *Soul & Spirit magazine*. I wouldn't have done any of these if I hadn't of wanted to impress the publishers so what started off as ego became such a beautiful way to help even more people with love. The next day after the winner was announced, I felt such a weight had lifted off my shoulders as I had surrendered the outcome and had fallen in love with the true purpose of writing this once again. I spent the day changing the chapters and channeling what needed to be in this book. The same day my manager had already got me a meeting with a different publisher. I opened myself up to whatever was for my highest good, and here this book is.

This whole experience has really helped me to trust myself so much more and trust that the Universe has an incredible plan for my love and I. I understand now that this all had to happen for the greater good. I've undergone so much transformation in these last few months and have awoken once again. I'm fulfilled, a being of light and love and I get to share that with my twin flame again. I feel like we're so much stronger now, more connected and more grateful for one another. So my message to you is to let go of what you think you need and let the Universe guide you to your dream life, it's a much smoother road if you do trust me! I was finally healed from my past and at peace with my future - I was living in the now.

'The wound is the place where
the Light enters you'
- Rumi

My best advice for dealing with your own controlling habits would be to really go within and find the root cause for WHY you want to manifest your desire. Mine were out of fear and as my spirit guides keep telling me 'It will happen when it's done out of love not out of ego'. I really began to examine my beliefs and needs for marriage, commitment and a book deal. They all essentially came down to the fear of not being loved, the fear of abandonment even with my twin flame. I thought I'd healed from my past wounds, but it was only when faced with my worst fear that I realised this was an opportunity for expansion and healing not some form of divine torture.

I also realised that I was putting myself on a society timeline of when I thought these key events in my life SHOULD happen and what everyone would think. I entered myself into some ego race and forgot the true nature of love and that time is an illusion we've created here on Earth. The key to accepting your path and spiritually surrendering is to be living entirely in the now. We only have today, tomorrow's not happened yet and yesterday is already done. These seem like simple reminders but essentially peace and freedom from our inner darkness is simple. We set up these barriers, blocks and limiting beliefs ourselves so coming out of them is easy, make peace with the now. I wasn't being grateful for the relationship I had right now or how far I'd already come in my career. I was living in the future and setting myself up for failure by doing so. Once again the time illusion had got the better of me and had installed over months this fear ridden desire that I HAD to have these big life events happen so soon otherwise...what? What would actually happen if I didn't get married, didn't get engaged or manifest shit tons of money. I'd still have my love, I'd still be happy, fulfilled and comfortable in life.

Nothing bad would happen from these manifestations not happening...this was all my ego. I'd been living in ego for months so no wonder the Universe shook things up and gave me an awakening. I believe my lesson here on this Earth is to learn self-love and independence. I'm always so worried that I won't have my happily ever after, but really why can't I have a happily ever now? I could buy myself a ring if I really wanted a ring on my finger. I could change my name if I really wanted to, fuck it I could buy myself my dream wedding dress right now just for the lols. I could even self-publish this book if I wanted to. None of what I wanted was out of love it was all materialistic ego bullshit. Hello ego I see you.

"Those who are certain of the outcome can afford to wait, and wait without anxiety."

—A Course In Miracles

Authentic Queen

The final journey of my path so far has been stepping into authenticity. What I mean by this is having spiritual confidence to share my experiences and views with the world. It's funny when I manifested a double page feature in *Soul & Spirit magazine* which actually ended up on the front cover with a picture of myself, I was asked to write all about spiritual confidence and how I had the balls to come out as a life coach at the age of twenty-four. This article really challenged me to think long and hard at actually what had given me this confidence throughout my career?

My spiritual sisters and I always joke about how much I'm in my divine masculine energy because I have the balls to do everything I put my mind to, no matter how impossible it may seem. I don't think it always stems from my own confidence personally, it stems from a deep knowing that by showing up to the world I'm being me. When I made the decision to re-brand away from *The Coupon Queen* it was a big scary moment. I did sit and think was I ready for this? Money-saving was all I knew and now I was stepping into the big world of self-help and spirituality as a baby really in comparison to the already established superstars in this field. What gave little Emma Mumford that confidence to say 'I'm here!'

Personally, I feel because I'm able to channel so well and clearly now, I think sometimes spirit takes over and is like 'Let's do this!' I had just attended a writer's course in Bristol and I thought 'I have to do this now'. What was I waiting for? So that evening I updated my website's domain, my logos, the whole brand and bought the trademark for 'Spiritual Queen'.

At first I doubted myself and thought would I ever be known as Emma after being under the Coupon Queen title for so long, that's all I was known for. Very quickly my followers got really excited and so did I. For once I was doing me! I had grown tired of *The Coupon Queen* and longed to just be Emma and now finally I was. I was able to talk freely about spirituality and be known for it. I then started contacting magazines to get featured and started up my podcast '*Spiritual Queen's Badass Podcast*'. At this point I had already been doing life coaching for a few months. When I started life coaching it was simply because someone asked me to help them. It started off as a few sessions, then more and more people started emailing me asking me if they could have a session. I had absolutely no idea what I was doing or why people were asking me. I ended up doing a life coaching course online and qualified as an 'Advanced Law of Attraction Practitioner'. This helped me because it gave me the structure and discipline I needed to help people.

Overtime, I had gained roughly around fifteen regular clients who I had sessions with every other week. I always received such great compliments about our sessions and testimonials that I enjoyed our sessions and it never truly felt like work. That's the beauty of what I do, even now writing this book is all out of passion and love. I do it because it makes me happy not for the money. Which leads me to my next topic. Knowing your worth in spirituality.

Charging money for your work can be rewarding and also tough. It got to a point where so many people where messaging me on Instagram asking for advice I had to draw the line. I was over worked and felt pressured to help all these people who couldn't afford coaching. It was then Marie Forleo's work came into my life, and she firmly taught me how to say no. Through her online videos I finally saw the worth in my own spiritual work and I learnt how to show people that they need to invest in themselves in the right way. I personally never messaged any of my spiritual idols I looked up to for advice, I did it myself and bought their work, books or courses and did the work myself because darling that's what your journey is. It's down to you to listen and take onboard advice you see or read - then action that. Now I'm not bashing the people who message me at all I love you all, but see your worth and understand that sometimes I don't have the time just like any other human. Our lives can be complex and situations you feel desperate about probably would take an hour session to explain and breakthrough together. I can't give you the support you deserve through a two-minute reply while on the way to lunch. You deserve better than that, you deserve my full attention. So understand that with any spiritual teacher/healer we're here to help in the correct setting.

If you're planning to go into spiritual teaching yourself, then this can be a tricky step. You don't want to disappoint people, but equally it's not filling your cup either. I don't think your mortgage provider will accept positive vibes and good karma as a monthly payment sadly. You need to look after yourself first, before you help others and that includes having food on your table. I do still reply to the odd message when I feel drawn to and help people, but people respect you so much more when you respect yourself.

I actually booked in with a life coach myself when I was going through a big spiritual lesson recently. The lady who I had been following online cost three times the amount I did an hour, but I 'invested' in myself. After the hour I felt strange as I felt like it hadn't benefited me at all. I just spoke for the hour, she didn't give me tools, advice, nothing. I had invested that money to realise my own worth. I knew from that point on I didn't need a life coach because I can help myself and how much value for money and content my clients get from my sessions.

A method to decide what you should charge for or do for free in your line of work, would be to ask yourself does it make me happy? If the answer is yes, do it. Happiness always leads to abundance and fulfilment, it doesn't matter where money comes from the Universe will always make sure you're looked after. It's all about reinstalling that trust and knowing by sharing your light into the world, the Universe will reward you. I've done quite a few freebies in my time, including contributing to magazines. I love writing don't get me wrong, but I was battling my ego in the sense I felt I should be charging for my articles as it was selling them copies. I'm such a preacher of know your own worth, that sometimes even I still get caught up on whether to work for free or not. Now I simply look at it as a great platform to launch my message. There will come a time where I'm not able to do all of these fun work commitments due to my schedule. So for now I'm extremely grateful for the opportunity and know that my work will reach even more people. I place my trust in the Universe that my needs will always be met, and I am abundant. It doesn't matter what business it comes through or for what service, the Universe will always surround me with its wealth (a great little one liner for you to repeat each morning in the mirror).

Anyway enough about money, my point is that you need to see your worth to have spiritual confidence. Many of my peers have commented about how I just seem to always be killin' it. Yes, I guess I am but that's because I've got to a stage where I wholeheartedly know why I'm here, my message, my purpose and at every stage I'm connected to the divine and trust what they give me. I take every opportunity that comes my way, I make mistakes, I learn. I believe in my passion, in my words and that I can help people. That wasn't always natural to me, I've built it up over time but you find once you get going the rest falls into place.

The next step of spiritual confidence comes from surrendering and trusting that you're exactly where you're meant to be right now. My path didn't start off with spirituality but it led me to exactly where I was meant to be. I trusted the Universe when it lead me to re-brand, I trusted every step as daunting and scary as it seemed at the time. I just did it, without a second thought and that's what leads to spiritual confidence. Now at every step I could have let my ego pipe up and say 'Emma you're a baby, there are much more qualified older teachers already in the world'. This is true there are but no one's going to tell it like I do and that's my superpower. I feel I'm here to awaken our souls younger, to help many my own age feel comfortable enough to speak up about spirituality and boldly step into their authentic self.

The best way to establish whether you should take a big leap in life or in your career would be to go within and vibe it. Whether that's using angel cards, meditation or asking for a sign, you already know the answer really. It's all about execution and making it happen. Again, this is probably why I manifest so easily because I take inspired action to make my dreams a reality every single day, without fail. It comes from a hunger within to serve, to help and to connect further with the divine. It's all about returning to love from fear based thoughts holding you back, and simply remembering the Universe wants you to succeed - it's routing for you!

Spiritual confidence does come with its struggles. There are times where I sit and think what next? I found power in admitting that my life had become one big checklist and it never should have been that way. I wasn't finding beauty in the journey and realising all that I had was the now. If you're anything like me I used to want everything now, the book deal, the seminars, you name it I've either already done it or I'm on the way to doing it. It took real strength to sit down and think 'Emma you have about sixty years left on this earth, fill your time wisely you don't need to do it all before kids'. We're always fearing time, either we're too young, too old, not this or not that. These are all irrelevant excuses we create to stop ourselves from executing our dreams - the truth is we create age, race, sexuality issues as to why we can't do something. What if that's your purpose though? Just like mine was to start this journey young to show people that age is just a number. So what limiting belief are telling yourself? Let's get real and eliminate that now!

The best way to really flourish into your spiritual confidence, is to be seen. Now what I mean by being seen, is being present. Being authentically you. So take some time to go within, and discover who you really are or who you'd like to be. Once you've discovered that - ask yourself are you being seen? Do you turn up to the Universe each and every day ready and willing to be of service? What I mean by service is - are you doing your spiritual routine in the morning (gratitude practise, meditation, Emotional Freedom Technique etc). Whatever you like to do in the morning to heighten your spirituality is showing up. If you don't show up each day how does the Universe know what you want? How does it know you're ready and willing to be of service to the divine and share light into the world.

By cultivating your own spiritual routine in the morning you'll carve the way for an abundant day and will be guided. At every given moment we're being guided by spirit, so trust this and know that you can have confidence in your journey. Are you showing love to all aspects of your life? This is also being seen. Are you working hard to nurture, uplift and inspire those around and share your light into their hearts. A lot of this may either seem simple or a strange way to build your own spiritual confidence. My point being that by showing up to the Universe each day you will notice your connection to the divine grow and more and more abundance flow into your life. This will give you confidence in your relationship with the Universe and allow you to trust the messages and signs you receive.

It's also about knowing when enough is enough - as empath's sometimes we always run to fix and heal people which is an incredible quality to be proud of. We must remember that we can't help everyone and that person must be wanting to help themselves first. You can't deplete yourself to fill someone else's cup, you need to make sure your relationships, friendships etc are being built together and expanding equally. If someone can't see your shine, worth or love - it's not your job to force them. Love doesn't need to be forced and remember you can't fix everyone it's just not our job and it will leave you feeling low and a failure because it hasn't worked. Let these people find their own inner strength - they're strong enough give them credit. You can support them when they are willing and open to love and support.

After re-branding and finding confidence in both myself and my work, it really grew rapidly. I then launched my own merchandise range which again was a big risk, investing money and designing my own products. I could feel my ego saying 'Who are you Emma to launch planners and self-help tools'. Exactly who was I? Emma of course, the woman who just keeps freakin' doing all these crazy things and it always helps people.

Making financial commitments can be scary because if it doesn't work out you're then left with stock and you lose your investment. No matter what, I had faith in my work and knew I was channeling what I needed to be in these products. My products to this day are doing incredibly well and although I'm only a year in, I'm already looking at hiring help to dispatch orders and keep up with demand. I trust my vision and just like this book the people who need it and it will help, will always find it.

The next step into being my authentic self was to say no to couponing press. Now this was hard as it earns me money and would have continued to grow my couponing brand until I sold it. I had to be really strict and remember that I was only doing what felt good from now on and money-saving didn't feel that good anymore.

I had cut all ties with Coupon Queen so I needed to follow through with this decision. Of course my ego piped up about growing my name and I worried about if it would affect the sale of the business, but I had to remember that if I wanted to be authentic and recognised as Emma by the Universe and by the public then I had to stay true to my work. As soon as I started saying no and handing these opportunities to other money saving bloggers, more abundance found me. I then found that I had the confidence to pitch to spiritual magazines, websites and they were accepting and publishing my work. This felt so much more fulfilling and grew my name more than any couponing press could have ever done. I was in alignment and trusting my journey.

My main message of this chapter is, what is done from love will always be a success. Success comes in many forms, and as long as you can do everything from a happy heart and from love it will always be done right. Nothing is ever a coincidence, so have faith that even if you've made mistakes in the past, that actually those mistakes were just leading you to this incredible future. What is meant for you will never pass you by. Sharing your light with the world and with your close circle will eventually open them up the love and light. So it's important that you remain seen and don't hide your spirituality away through fear or judgement. Together we are here to share the light among this world and remove all illusion and fear until we are left with love of the purest forms. Your nearest and dearest may judge you, they may make fun and not understand it. My parents and friends called me weird. Now they're all on the positivity bandwagon. The more you step into your authentic self they will have no choice but to look up to you, and equally do the same. It's all energy remember, like attracts like. Authenticity attracts authenticity in the people and circumstances around you.

Stepping out and admitting my biggest fears was scary but incredibly liberating. When I witnessed the shadow within me and accepted my past mistakes, lies and fear based actions, I set myself free from illusion and fear. I've always been good at letting my own mistakes go (or so I thought), but terrible at forgiving others. I soon realised this in my twin flame, that he was holding a mirror up to me and what I couldn't forgive in him was actually what I couldn't forgive within myself. My biggest fear is not being loved, and I think this is what has motivated me from a young age to be successful in life.

When I spiritually awakened back in 2016 I thought I had this nailed and had forgiven and let go of my past. I was so eager to please when I was younger, I fell into the wrong crowds and could never be my true self around anyone because truthfully I never understood myself. I did some pretty irresponsible and rebellious things growing up, but do you know what, I wouldn't change that for the world. It showed me my ultimate fear and allowed me to witness this all these years later. I was only ever hurting myself by not stepping into my authentic self.

So when I suddenly saw of all my love's flaws were actually a deep rooted fear within me I had never truly witnessed...bam it hit me so hard. It was like I knew all of this but once again I was remembering. It was time for me to address these fears once and for all and step into my authentic self. If I couldn't hold my hands up to my own errors, secrets, past trauma, and witness it how would I heal? I started by writing down all the issues we had, I then turned it into a personal statement and sat with it. There in its full glory was everything I was running from.

It's funny I always felt like I was authentic and honest, but there was still a few hidden gems I hadn't healed yet. When we allow ourselves to address our past, our flaws and sit with them, something magical happens - we open up the door to healing. When we witness these acts of ego and fear we are present, whole and most importantly authentically us. So what haven't you addressed? Do you feel worthy of spiritual confidence? I ended up telling my spiritual sisters these truths as it helped me to heal and know I would never be judged. My sisters are my support unit and I knew we had created a safe space where judgement didn't exist, and we could all confess fear based mistakes we had made in our pasts. Revealing this felt like a weight had been lifted. I was ready to be 100% authentically me and confident in my spiritual path.

As a light worker, hiding shadow would never let me truly shine. So do yourself a favour babe, forgive yourself and shine brighter. We all make mistakes, we all learn that's simply the process of life - that's our human side. We can't beat ourselves up for acts we committed before being consciously aware of our actions and self-love. There is no such thing as perfection otherwise how else would we learn? So witness your shadow, sit with and most importantly share it in a safe place if you can, among your tribe. Holding onto these things never helps and we all hold on to events and situations that just don't matter and all equal a state of fear and illusion.

Ego Queen

I first learnt about dissolving the ego through twin flame work. While my love and I were in the runner/chaser stage of our twin flame union I realised so many of the problems he had were actually problems within me (it's like they hold up one big mirror to you). Also that for twins to come into full harmonious union they had to dissolve the ego and face their fears. I first dissolved my ego when I spiritually awakened two years prior, I felt like I was bossin' this ego stuff, well if you've read the previous chapter you'll know I clearly had the work to do again!

I don't feel we can ever truly wave goodbye to our egos but what we can do is show them love and compassion. I always see my ego as my inner child, crying out in panic and trying to protect me from things going wrong. Essentially that's all the ego is...it's protecting you. So don't bash your ego or make it feel like an intruder. It's a part of you just like your soul and just like you it needs to feel love. First of all I want to do this little exercise with you, this is one of the many tools I use with my life coaching clients which I learnt from Julia Cameron's work.

1. What would you name your ego? - Think of the first name that comes into your head as silly as it may sound.

2. What are the qualities of your ego? - Are they rude, pessimistic, sexist etc..

3. Who in your life is (name of your ego) - I love this step as so many people soon realise that actually their

ego is someone in their life either past or present. It can also be more than one person.

My ego's name is Charlie. He is sexist, rude and very belittling of my happiness. Charlie reminds me of my Dad and the male figures I used to have in my life like old bosses. Now my Dad is a lovely person don't get me wrong I love him to pieces, but in the past he has always doubted my happiness and made me second guess my intuition for a more 'realistic' approach. These men in my life have all driven me to successfully be in my divine masculine, it's nothing to be ashamed of, it's why I'm such a hard worker and have achieved so much so young. The problem is finding my balance and finding my divine feminine energy. We all should have a balance of both in our life and realising this was a great call to embrace my divine feminine energy.

Charlie and I have such a love hate relationship, while he's learnt to trust me and my intuition over time, guess what he still likes to creep in and make me believe he's acting from love. So let's get really real about the ego. Once you've established who in your life represents your ego ask yourself has this person ever been right about you? Has anything they've ever said to you been true? I can guarantee the answer is no. So why do we give these egos qualifications, it's like we install all this trust in something that has absolutely no qualifications at all. I mean it's like a psychic for example, if you were looking to go to one and found someone online you'd look at their reviews. If you read bad reviews of clients saying how awful their accuracy was would you go to them? So let's say you do and they tell you all about your Uncle Jeff from Cardiff, but the truth is you don't have an Uncle Jeff... then the psychic carries on to tell you that you shouldn't go for that job because it won't end well. Now are you seriously telling me you'd trust that shit? So how on earth is this any different from installing our trust in our ego.

Whoever your ego represents, they have more than likely told you some negative, character crushing opinions in your lifetime which has left your ego feeling bashed and bruised. It's okay because your ego needs love that's all. Now you've established that there is no truth in the ego, and that it's all illusion you can tend to it. Think of your ego as your inner child, and just think how scared it is for you as these bad things happened in the past. Your ego loves you and wants to protect you from harm, it's your job to nurture your ego and show it that it needn't fear or worry because you're in control and you'll make sure everything will be okay. The Universe has your back at all times. So you don't need to rely on ego, return to love.

If you feel your ego is holding onto situations or going into overdrive then write a list of every circumstance it's worrying about. Really analyse why you're holding onto them, just like my book deal I couldn't be at peace because my ego was in play. It wanted the fame, the money, the validation and to feel loved. It didn't possibly want to face its darkest fear of not being loved, therefore it took the steering wheel and tried to force the publishers to love me. The truth was the Universe had a better plan and as soon as I surrendered and showed my ego love the abundance poured in.

The way to show your ego love is to nurture your inner child. Establish your deepest darkest fear - mine was the fear of not being loved. Think back to the first time you felt that fear. Mine was as a small child. Play back that event in your mind and speak to your inner child, tell your inner child what it would have wanted to hear. Mine would have been that I was loved no matter what and it was all illusion.

As children we grow and learn, sometimes we create these stories which seem so real to us when in fact they're all illusion. We carry these traumas into our relationships and adulthood and this is what causes our ego to be in full season. I was loved as a child, but at that time I felt that as an only child that I never really had someone of my own – I had a fear of not being loved. My parents were always a strong unit, but I never felt involved in that unit. That was all illusion. Through school I never really had a best friend, but I had friends. In my previous relationships they were all so family orientated and I never felt a partnership or part of anything. That was my problem I didn't have someone to call my own throughout my life, so no wonder my ego needed to feel loved and thought it wouldn't get it's happily ever after. I always was loved though. This is how young Emma chose to see the world and then put herself through years of pain not seeing the bigger picture. So it's time to love yourself even more and especially Charlie.

I personally love to do EFT (Emotional Freedom Technique). I have watched numerous YouTube videos on letting go, releasing fear and worry, self-love, being in the now, inner child healing and healing in general. All of these help the ego and anything linked to your deepest fear will help also. I'm also a big advocate of mirror work, so I always address Charlie or little Emma and put my hands on my heart. I will look in the mirror into my eyes and say 'Emma I love you, I really really love you and you are surrounded by such genuine people who love you so much'.

Tailor these affirmations to your fears or just free style. Sometimes I just ramble on to Charlie and reassure him that no matter what happens I've got us and we have each other. If you feel your ego resisting then keep sending it love every time it pipes up throughout the day, they just need reassurance. It will take a few weeks for your ego to trust you and to trust this love, so keep being persistent and loving. Trust yourself you've got this! Befriend your ego, become best friends, that's how you work in harmony when your inner child/ego can trust that you've got this. Even if you feel like you haven't got your shit together what would you say to your own children if they were worried? You wouldn't cry on the floor saying you don't know what to do. You stay strong, you show them love and you work out the rest as you go along - you show them no fear. This is how you work with ego, love them, nurture them and praise them because they actually have your best interests at heart, they are just scared and project failure in hopes you don't make a risky decision - it's all about playing it safe.

So let's move on to projection. I'll use my Dad as an example for this one - my ego reminds me of my Dad because of how realistic and prepared he always is for every outcome. My Dad's had an interesting life and had been married previously.

He's suffered heartache and I certainly get my romantic nature from him. The fact that Dad has been hurt with love means he's projected that onto me. Now as a Dad he wanted to protect me and make sure I didn't get hurt. That's all any parent wants for their child, but his projections and his ego had lead me to create this ultimate fear of not being loved.

So I want you to understand that no matter what your egos (people who represent them) have said to you, they are projecting their own life experiences onto you. These people were doing the best they could, so remember that no matter how nasty they've been to you or how many scars they've left. Forgive them. When I need to do some forgiveness work I like to write statements like this -'Dad I forgive you for projecting a fear of trusting love onto me, because you've been hurt before and I understand you wanted to protect me'. Writing these statements can be so healing for you both and allows you to escape victim mode and return to a place of love. I would also really encourage you to do some Angelic chord cutting meditations which you can find online, to cut these negative ties with these people who represent your ego. Now I know it may seem dramatic especially if it's a parent, but it's important to only allow a positive stream of energy to flow between you both. So chord cutting isn't killing anyone off, it's protecting your energy and allowing if you choose to a new positive stream of energy to flow between you both.

Like with all negativity, when someone calls you names, or is just damn rude about you, know it isn't true. All negativity stems from projection, a deep rooted fear in that individual. Take my ex for example, after we'd split and he ran off with his new woman. I got my life back on track, I focused on myself and on my career. He hated this and probably realised what a mistake he'd made. So he started spreading around that I was lying about what happened and then hacked my website while I was on national TV. He posted a message saying 'This website is unavailable because I'm a stuck up bitch'. Thanks for that. Now why did he do this?

Well the only logic I can find in this was he was so unhappy with his own life, that he hated seeing me do well without him. He hated the fact that I was living and breathing on my own and doing SO much better without him. He hated my success and that I was going somewhere. He knew being on *This Morning* was my dream so wanted to tarnish that. That is all negativity is essentially, projection of the other person's insecurities. So please understand that what these people have told you isn't true. We all have different life paths and experiences, so although my Dad wanted to protect me from harm he actually made it worse by fuelling my ego. He didn't want me to get my hopes up about love, and to always expect the worse after his hopes had been crushed numerous times. The truth is I have my own destiny and my heart was going to get broken before I met my twin flame, that had to happen to get me here. But an act of love turned into a hatred of men and a fear of not being loved. My Dad was doing the best he could and so are your people. Send them love, they need it the most. Forgive them and set yourself free from this fear you've gripped onto for too long.

The key to maintaining peace with your ego is to keep checking in with yourself. Always ask yourself when manifesting are you wanting this from love or ego? Anytime you feel your ego cropping up send it love and reassure it. Work on your trust with the Universe. Do you feel supported and in alignment? The Universe has got you baby so it's time to take your hands and your ego's hands off the steering wheel of life and see where the Universe is taking you! Love your inner Charlie, love your inner child, it is possible to all work together and to most importantly listen to your soul. As I once read in Kyle Gray's fantastic book *Light Warrior* FEAR - Forgive Everyone And Release.

"When I'm in alignment with the love of the Universe, peace cannot be disrupted"

—Gabrielle Bernstein

Light Queen

Letting in the light may seem the most obvious thing to do during your spiritual journey, yet so many of us resist this when obstacles occur in our life. A powerful memory of me letting the light back in, was when my love and I were apart for the second time when I found the power of my thoughts and words. I had surrendered, felt like I had let go, was totally calm, peaceful but I just lacked something. Nothing felt as good without him. Now normally that sounds like something out of a movie. My love could not complete me, any lack was lack within myself and I don't know why after all my awakenings, realisations, and breakthroughs, even spirit literally telling me 'You're 100% getting back with him chill'. I had a doubt in me, something I was resisting and I couldn't work out what it was.

I had my incredible psychic Rachel who has been 99.9% accurate about everything in my life, tell me way before that we'd be married, this is the one and I even knew that in myself. I'd predicted our two week break, and like clockwork predicted everything and boom we got back together. I think because I didn't see this coming it hit me harder, I couldn't feel a sense of time or why this was happening so it scared me. I knew it would finally end all cycles, we'd heal and be happy together once again...so why was I unhappy? I'd absolutely nailed this last time round, got in such a high vibe and was having so much fun the two weeks flew past. I had realised that I probably wasn't letting go as much as I thought I had and should surrender once again and let the Universe guide me.

I had a real and frank talk with my ego and asked 'What are you fearing?' and it replied 'That he won't come back this time'. This seemed silly, I had been shown numerous signs, messages, white butterflies, I felt with my whole being it wasn't the end so what was my ego doing?!

Something was different this time and I couldn't work out why I just couldn't have faith. I did a powerful creation meditation by Gabrielle Bernstein as the time before I did this and received incredible guidance. Once again, I had a beautiful message from a spirit channeling through me, it was loving, supportive and even told me within 11 days we'd be back in union. Hello! I'd just been told a time frame, and exactly what I sensed myself and yet that still didn't give me a warm fussy feeling inside. They gave me hope, they gave me every piece of information my controlling ego would want to hear, but still Charlie was not satisfied. So I got real I said to my ego 'Okay well let's let go then - let's call myself single, take down the photos and move on'. To which I felt a horrible feeling and Charlie replied 'No, that doesn't feel right you're together'. I then said 'Okay then, let's move on and manifest our real husband' and it replied 'No because it's him'. So my ego even knew the truth, but what on earth was it resisting. I then realised it was my faith in the Universe. The Universe had never let me down before now, but I did feel let down. No matter how bad my past was I got through it and I knew greater things awaited, so why couldn't I feel that now? I began to feel upset, and worried because no one saw this coming and although Rachel, Angels, spirit guides and even my own intuition were like 'You're fine it's all going to work out and be glorious' I couldn't feel that.

My faith in the Universe had been tested, I trusted it whole heartedly with every other aspect of my life, but not my relationship for some reason. I wasn't in control, my ego hated that it couldn't sense a time, that there was no contact. Charlie was scared. I continued to do spiritual practises but nothing shifted this heavy feeling on my heart. I raised my vibes, I had fun, but nothing would fix this lack of faith and hope.

I began to hear *'All of Lights'* by Kayne West play in mind constantly for days, I thought it was such a random song I hadn't heard in years and what did it mean? I went to bed that evening feeling again confused as to why I doubted what I knew in my heart and soul I deserved. Earlier in the day I had replaced the lights behind my bed for my YouTube background, and had put up net lights instead and hung photos of my loved ones on it. I put the old lights on my drawers and went to bed. I woke up around 2am and saw these lights were turned on...I didn't think anything of it and thought 'Oh it's not that bright I'll turn it off in the morning', even though these lights hadn't been turned on by me! I then woke back up to see the lights now flashing, and once again I hadn't turned them on or changed the mode. What was happening? It felt loving though, it didn't feel creepy or negative.

So the next morning I woke up and thought what the hell happened last night? I Googled the spiritual meaning of lights turning on and it was all to do with Angels. This website spoke about how it's your Angels giving you hope, faith and want you to know your desire is being handled.

It's also a call to let in the light....boom there it was. I wasn't letting in the light and allowing the Universe's love and abundance to wash over my fears. I then listened to Kayne West's song and once again was like I need to let the light in! I then left my music playing on shuffle as I got ready, and most of the songs reflected being on the right path, letting the light shine and having what I desire. Wow. Hello Angels!

I don't know what had lead me to this place, but I let the light back in and surrendered to the Universe once again. I needed it's help to reinstall my hope and faith. My ego was in fear mode and didn't want to accept my intuition and how I'd been right 100% of my life, all of the signs, angel cards, the 18726 white butterflies appearing everywhere, the name of my love and his higher self's name appearing everywhere. I mean let's be real my ego was being like a spoilt child in a sweet shop, kicking off and screaming on the floor. 'I know I'll get these sweets after dinner (divine timing), but I want them now!' Ladies and gentleman my ego everyone! It's not wrong for me to want love, I'd met the love of my life you would expect that. The truth is a twin flame journey is an awakening one and it's not easy until you come into full union and dissolve your egos. I was learning so much about myself and twin flame there was so much more to this separation than simply us arguing. Heck I spiritually awoke again!

By letting in the light and surrendering I let the love of the Universe wash over me. I released the pain and heaviness I'd been carrying on my shoulders, and just said 'You've got this Universe I have no other option than to trust you now, just like I have many times before now and I know no matter what's meant for me will always find me. I hand this over to you and ask that you remind me of the love that surrounds me, universal love, continue to show me hope and strength and deliver me to my destiny with grace and certainty'.

I know I've already covered the importance of spiritually surrendering but do you know what handing that baton back over the to the Universe after being worn down, felt liberating and the right thing to do. Immediately after doing this, so much love washed over me, and I saw even more signs reminding me of my love. When we invite the light into the wound, healing can begin.

We are guided, we are no longer lost or feel uncertain. As when you return to love, you feel grounded and can hear your intuition further. It doesn't matter if we didn't sense this obstacle coming, we're not meant to know everything up front. That's the beauty of life we were sent here to face these obstacles and overcome each and every one with strength and beauty. That's the miracle, not the end result - the awakening you experience during your healing. I was waiting on the return of my love to be a miracle, but that was just an eventuality. The miracle was my realisation of my actions, my words, my return to love, healing my ego and letting the light back in. It's okay to tell the Universe you're struggling, we all do it. That's why we have kickass Angels, spirit guides, fairies etc to guide us along our journey. My Angels had my back and seeing those fairy lights light up by themselves in the middle of the night showed me that anything IS possible, and that I can trust everything I was seeing and hearing.

The way to let the light in, is to simply invite it in. You can do this through meditation, a ritual which could simply be lighting a candle and speaking with the Universe. There are many personal ways to connect with your Angels, spirit guides and the Universe. The best way is through intention and simply starting the conversation. We don't have to go through this journey alone, that's why you're reading my book, other great light workers' books, watching videos online and receiving guidance from the universe. We're all in the same boat and share our experiences so that you too can let in the light. Accepting the light not only reminds you that you are already whole, perfect and just freaking amazing - it shows you your truth, reminds you of your essence and allows you to thrive.

Finding acceptance for the now is also a powerful way to invite the light into your life. So often we give up our power and light to circumstances out of our control, we fight and fight when actually by floating we become calm and present. I always share my analogy of looking calm on the surface but struggling (resisting) underneath the water. If we only stopped and allowed ourselves to float, the current (Universe) will deliver us to our shore (destiny) far quicker and peacefully rather than drowning in the sea alone.

Sometimes faith isn't enough, just like me the Universe was literally giving me ALL the certainty I needed but I was too busy struggling underneath the water to receive that and feel peace. I needed to stop, stand still and appreciate the now. Find the miracles in the present moment, stop living in the past, or future. Yes, my twin flame was here to break every cycle and he was coming back, but I was simply depriving myself of the beauty of today, depriving myself of love and stopping myself from living my best life. If you can't find gratitude in the now, how can the Universe bring you even more abundance?

The way to let in the light, is to work on your self-love once again. Open up your heart chakra through a guided meditation, through mirror work, through dancing to your favourite music, by doing you. Reclaim your power and surrender to the Universe. Surrender your agenda and ask for that help. By surrendering to the divine and letting go and loving ourselves we open up the path for the Universe to deliver our miracles. We step out of the way and the Universe can get to work. Nothing feels better than letting the light back in and remembering your power. You are an incredible soul and you deserve to worship yourself, you have got yourself through 100% of the obstacles and hardships in your life. So you will 100% be able to face anything that comes your way now or in the future. Give yourself the credit, give yourself the time to heal and most importantly surrender.

Now you'd think by surrendering you're losing your desire or you feel the Universe won't think you want it anymore. This is such an illusion, you actually tell the Universe you're ready for it by surrendering because you're totally present and in the now. You're not living in the past, you're not living in the tomorrow, you're here, right here and right now. That's when the Universe can truly get to work. By opening up my heart chakra, loving myself and truly surrendering my will to the Universe. I kid you not the weird feeling totally disappeared. My love then contacted me for the first time in over a week with a loving response. That's the real power of love, self-love.

I could finally appreciate the signs and messages the Universe was bringing me. Although it wasn't quite the reunion yet, I was instantly reminded by spirit that everything was as they had planned and nothing had changed. I felt a wave of peace wash over me, even though it wasn't the message I wanted I was at peace. I continued on with my day and every time I saw signs for him, I just said 'Thank you Universe for reminding me to love myself more'. I was once again aligned, full of love, and in tune with my truth.

It was really important for me to keep working on my heart chakra during this time, to make sure I was forgiving myself, him and most importantly opening up the all the love that surrounded me in the present. I had to totally accept my situation currently and find the joy and love in the now. It was a call to love myself more, and to radiate love out into the world. There was no way he could resist that strong, independent, divine feminine vibe! By doing these meditations each day, which can be found on YouTube easily, I opened up my heart, instead of closing it off and avoiding pain. My heart wanted to close off and feel numb, but why? There was absolutely nothing to fear.

I'd already proven I could manifest him then again and it would happen again for good this time. There are only positives to letting the light in, because darling you start to realise that miracles happen daily and occur naturally.

Now if you're anything like me then you would have perceived miracles to be the manifestation coming into fruition. Wrong! Miracles are shifts in perception. Let's think about that - what if a manifestation was simply an after effect of a miracle? A certain reward for all your hard work, personal development and faith? This is how I now view manifestations. The REAL miracle comes from your breakthroughs, realisations and growth.

Your journey can reveal so many incredible things to you. Think about how far you've come in all of this, the hurdles you've overcome, and the positive impact you've made not only in your life but others too. Think back to six months ago even a year ago - think about how far you've come and what blessings have entered your life. THAT is the miracle. I want to stress this because I totally believed that in receiving my desires my questions would be answered. The truth was they weren't the answers and that's because I wasn't honouring my journey and acknowledging the miracle was actually in the journey. I was tolerating the journey and not finding the beauty in the now. The most important relationship in our life is the one we have with ourselves, that's the only answer we ever need. So once I allowed the light in and realised that enjoying the now didn't mean the Universe was slowing down my desires at all, it was really speeding them up. By getting up each day, getting on with it, shining my light, keeping myself occupied, being productive, and doing everything I would have done normally - that was the secret to success. Not letting anything tarnish my incredible experience of life and self-love.

Now I know I haven't covered what happened here in my relationship fully, but by doing all of the above and just totally becoming the person I was at the beginning of the relationship, happy, carefree and full of self-love I was irresistible to him. I didn't have to force anything.

Although we didn't speak much during this time apart, my vibes were getting to him and he could feel how strong and full of happiness I was. That's the power of the Universe babes, your vibes can travel anywhere! I eventually didn't care what day he came back to me, I knew this time was allowing him to heal and myself. I had time to write this book, discover more about myself, have fun with my friends, and appreciate the calm and tranquility of my life. There was absolutely no lack in my life, only love. I gave up all expectations of us being back together for our one year anniversary and totally surrendered to the Universe.

I was so busy enjoying life, having fun and creating this book that when it did happen it totally took me by surprise and I loved that! By releasing my firm grip on it having to be him, I gave him the time to heal and love himself again. I realised this was the kindest thing to do, let him find himself and he would eventually find me again if it was meant to be. I had upgraded spiritually, found the beauty in the now, dissolved my ego, let the light in, wrote this kick ass book, created other incredible ideas for my business and appreciated this time in my life. THAT was the miracle. One day it won't just be me, when we live together I'll be around him more, then our children will come along. I finally started appreciating this peaceful time to discover myself, be with myself and love myself even more. I faced my biggest fear of letting my dream man go knowing that at the right time he would return and we would have the most incredible relationship again.

By finally releasing my grip on manifesting him back again and floating with this situation I was enjoying life. It didn't matter anymore whether he did come back or not because either way I knew I was happy and loved. Surely enough as soon as I started living and breathing this belief, the Universe got to work quickly. There was such a higher purpose to ALL of this happening, the struggles and pain were all worth it for him to heal, finally love himself, all of my miracles and realisations. Us being in harmonious union was simply an after effect of all the miracles we had encountered in our own spiritual growth. Now that's a shit ton of miracles baby!

Victim Queen

I want to talk about the dreaded victim mode. You may or may not have heard of this term before, but if you haven't then it's time I introduced you. Victim mode can become the killer of all dreams, sometimes we find ourselves blaming others for circumstances and situations out of 'our' control. For instance I used to be in victim mode about my ex-boyfriend because he left me with the flat, debt and ran off with another girl. I sat in victim mode for weeks and oh boy it felt good! To blame him, to be higher than him and in full blown Beyonce *'Best Thing You Never Had'* mood! Yeah that soul-crushing few weeks felt fucking great until my bubble was popped by the Universe.

The Universe showed me that actually Emma, you did have a part in that break-up, although I didn't deserve those things to happen to me I was using them to feed my ego and fall further into depression. Now there will be a few of you reading this who have been through incredibly traumatic things in your life, especially as children which of course you didn't have a human part in, you didn't deserve it and I send you all the loving healing light I can because you're so loved. It's not about saying you deserved it at all, taking yourself out of victim mode is understanding WHY these things happen to us.

If you're playing the blame game, you're avoiding all the healing and lessons the Universe wants you to have. Before we come here to Earth, as souls I imagine us all sitting round a big table planning our lives, our relationships, jobs, houses, heartaches, lessons and ultimately, we choose everything that happens to us in life. We choose our parents, our family, every single aspect of our lives, including our lessons - these are our soul missions. Soul missions are what we come here to learn. Mine I believe at this point, but I'm sure it will evolve with time, is to realise self-love is the most important relationship in life and to teach spirituality to the world.

By avoiding our soul mission, we're just not helping ourselves out at all! We're just prolonging the healing process and living in a spiral of lack and hurt which really doesn't manifest anything. I want you to have a look at your situation with me, so answer these questions on this page or in a notebook -

Who are you blaming?

What are you blaming them for?

What is stopping you from forgiving this person/situation?

What have you learnt since this situation arose?

Why do you think this had to happen?

Looking at your answers above, how do you feel now? Sometimes evaluating the situation like this can take us straight out of victim mode and into the miracle realisation that everything happens for a reason. I want you to know that the Universe is all loving for you and would never punish you. Nothing is ever lost, everything is merely transformed in this life and the Universe will never leave you lacking anything. We chose these hardships, these pains and mountains to climb - but baby that's where the good stuff is at. Completing our soul missions, learning those valuable lessons and growing as a soul. This is our classroom and we won't stop learning until our last breath.

It's easy for us to fall into victim mode, because as positive spiritual beings who emit love and light into the world, why do these shit things happen to us? Forgiveness is the best policy here. When you forgive the person who has wronged you, you actually set both of you free. I've known people who have written letters to their abusive ex's and got everything out on this paper they needed to and were then able to move on, release their blocks and live an incredible life. Now I'd only suggest doing this if it's safe to do so, you can just write the letter and burn it afterwards to also show a sign of forgiveness and letting go. It's important that you tell the person why you forgive them, the lessons they've taught you and heck you could even thank them! If you feel this is too far fetched right now I would suggest also calling in Archangel Michael to help cut the chords between you and this person. Imagine him cutting the energetic chord between you and this person with his great sword. Also, ask Archangel Michael to help you forgive this person and see them through the eyes of love. This can be a process, but forgiveness is an instant way out of victim mode and back into the abundant alignment of love.

Now I know some of you will be thinking that you can't find anything to be grateful for about this situation or to actually take any responsibility yourself. So, I want to show you an example with my ex-boyfriend. I wasn't taking responsibility for the fact I was unhappy in that relationship I just kept going, hurting myself even more. I let him walk over me and lowered my standards to have him in my life. I neglected my own needs, worth and self-love to fit in with him and his family. I hated his way of life as it was so far from my purpose, but I neglected my own goals to please him. I allowed myself to be treated like shit, spoken to like shit by his family and I didn't stand up for myself. I had withdrawn my love knowing how unhappy I was but stayed in that relationship way longer than I should have.

It's also about being a bit kinder to yourself and gentle, sometimes even after finding forgiveness for others we don't feel immediately free. This can be because most importantly we're not forgiving ourselves for what happened also. As easy as it is to blame others - we too can hold onto that blame unnecessarily. So make sure to find all the reasons why you can forgive yourself also. I beat myself up for staying longer than I should have - but I loved him and that's something to be proud of that I didn't just give up straight away. It doesn't matter how long it takes you to realise something, leave or do the right thing - everything is as it should be. Sometimes we have to go back to those relationships, friendships, workplaces to learn something extra before we can finally walk away. There is no right or wrong answer here only love. So make sure you're being loving to yourself here and not holding onto blame.

You can see that even I can find my responsibility in that situation even if it was minimal. Now two years on I can think of even more amazing lessons that situation has taught me and all the abundance that was awaiting me afterwards. It's time to step out of victim mode, you've stayed in there long enough dwelling. Take ownership of your responsibility, forgive the person or situation and let it all go. You can take strength from the lessons you've been presented with and know that now you will never let this happen to you again. It's about turning your rock bottoms into your success story just like I've done. Take this pain and turn it into motivation and drive to heal yourself and help others. That's your miracle, following your soul mission.

"Darkness cannot drive out darkness; only light can do that. Hate cannot drive out hate; only love can do that."

—Martin Luther King, Jr.

Energy Queen

Through learning about the Law of Attraction we all do energy work every single day. When we set an intention, when we speak into existence or visualise something manifesting into our reality - this is all energy work.

Through connecting with my spirit guides on a deeper level during this journey they have shown me how energy work can really help us positively manifest and more effectively. During my twin flame separation a visualisation came to me one day of us sat in an infinity symbol. One side of the circle was mine, the other his and we sat in the middle facing one another. I could see grass in each of our halves mine was very green, neat and the flowers looked healthy and vibrant. On his half of the circle the grass and flowers looked overgrown and dry. It was only after a few visits to this visualisation during meditation I realised I had created my own energy space to manifest with him. While we both ran away from our connection I could see us going around our circles chasing and running from one another. Yet once I had grasped that if I stayed still, peaceful and present in the middle he would eventually come and sit in front of me and do the same. This is classic Law of Attraction whatever we put out we attract back and very true of twin flames as we mirror one another.

Once I had found this life hack - when I saw us sat peacefully in the middle communication love and peace within days he would return and reflect this peace and love. Although some of the running was karmic and needed to happen both ends I kept coming back to this practise, turning my back to my side of the circle when I needed to and focused on -

nurturing my garden (self), sometimes he'd creep up behind me and be ready other times I had to be patient and wait for divine timing. Energy work like this can be really powerful and I have certainly seen situations and people shift using these methods. I also always call upon Archangel Michael & Archangel Raphael to stand with us helping to heal and protect us. This is really important with energy work as I'm about to show you.

I remember being sat in a restaurant in London with my good friend Hannah feeling funky that my love and I were having troubles without any explanation as it had been going so well and I had been doing my work. All of a sudden I had this powerful intuition that someone in my friend group had been sending bad energy our way, wanted me to be miserable and was jealous of me. I knew exactly who this was and they we're sneaky as hell. I told Hannah this and she agreed I should listen to my intuition and not feel crazy. The more I witnessed this I could see all the puzzle pieces coming together and it suddenly made sense. I couldn't believe it can this stuff be real?! How can someone send bad vibes and it actually be keeping us apart.

These are also more commonly known as psychic attacks. What I would like to stress is that this happening was karmic this won't happen to everyone and I certainly don't want you to fear this - I believe educating people on recognising the signs is vital and will prevent this from happening to others. These people knew exactly what they were doing, but sometimes bad vibes can be sent to us unintentionally by a jealous or bitter party. Energy can only affect us like this if there is room for it, most jealousy and bad vibes will bounce off you if you maintain a high vibration and not let energy vampires drain you. This is essentially what these people were doing, they found out my weakness - him and our separation. Posed as a friend and mentor and did this all behind the scenes.

The positive here is that this was karmic so this had to happen which did restore my faith in the Universe as I did find myself asking how this could all happen? Also, once you witness energy vampires effecting your life the energy stops immediately. That night Hannah and I did lots of chord cutting, commanding the energy to be sent back to its original source and clearing using Archangels, Ascended Masters, Starseeds, White Dragons basically we had to call the whole gang in to help shift this heavy cloud over me. Once we had it was like I could breathe again, Hannah also felt the energy and was like this is crazy!

Then the weirdest thing happened I had the most intense cold, cough and flu for about a week which is a classic sign of energy releasing. I had to rest and a lot of emotions came up, it was honestly like I was recovering from an illness. I want to stress this was an extreme case with people who knew what they were doing. This is very unlikely to happen to you but if after the techniques you feel you still need to shift something I would advise working with a mentor you feel connected with to help you remove this energy.

During this purging of energy I began to see my twin flame through the eyes of love, all past negativity and blame has simply vanished. I mean it was just bizarre how this energy had created the illusion of hate and separation between us both. During this time I began to see the energy vampires in my life who were enjoying my misery and jealous of my work. I had to do this whole process again with others too. I was in shock that people so close to me could do this but as I stated an energy vampire will normally be jealous and bitter and this is what creates the bad vibes, most will just be enjoying your misery. Some classic signs of someone sending you bad energy or a psychic attack is you feel drained, you may get headaches, you may feel tired, things go wrong for no reason, your appearance may even change for example my acne got really bad or you may even get pains in your body.

These attacks can vary in length some last hours, days, weeks mine from numerous sources lasted nearly a year. It's important to stress though I didn't know this was happening for a long while until the term popped into my life - then it was almost like a lightbulb moment.

After witnessing this energy my whole life changed I was able to speak up, speak my truth and reclaim my power. Suddenly everything with my twin improved, although not straight away in the psychical energetically all the blockages, hurdles and problems simply disappeared. The space was clear, it was over - the hardships were over. I received messages from his higher self, my spirit guides, and past loved one's that we were free to be together now and the worst was over - no one was influencing us now only our own energy.

From here I always imagine our infinity symbol surrendered by a white light, I call upon Archangels and can do our energy work surrounded by love and light. The important thing to remember is that all energy work must be done for the highest good if you're asking for you partner or friend to do something in the psychical ask for this 'or something better for the highest good'. Remember there is still free will at play here and you can't force anything on anyone who wouldn't want that anyway. Surely it would be much better that this person did whatever it is because they wanted to. It did take some time for everything to re-align but witnessing these energy vampires was so important. I know this may seem scary but as long as all energy work is done for the highest good and with love and light you are protected and it will work. Whether that's with your significant other, twin flame, family or friends. Personally I'm really visual and for my relationship this visual really helped me - energy work can also be done simply with words and intention just like manifesting. Just always include - as long as it's for the highest good!

Some signs that you have an energy vampire in your life would be to look at who doesn't support you 100% - for me it was the people who didn't support our relationship, my work or enjoyed seeing me miserable about our time apart. These vampires can be sneaky as hell so I would really invite you to look at everyone in your life and assess who has your back and who is secretly wanting you to fail. You will always be able to tell, and their true colours do come out eventually and your intuition will always know. As I said earlier ensuring their negativity doesn't affect you is really simple.

1. Witness It

When we acknowledge the people in our lives who are putting us down, trying to convince us of their bullshit or just have a problem with everything we do in life. These are your vampires. If you can look at your life and say that everyone has your best interests at heart and do support you wholeheartedly in a positive way - I want you to throw yourself a party because you are incredibly blessed! Don't worry if you can't it's easy to blame ourselves in this situation for letting these people in but like myself it could be karmic - it was always meant to happen. Heck I obviously had to write this chapter so no wonder it happened so I could talk about the positive and negative side of energy. It's also important to stress we are ALL doing energy work every single day with manifesting - every thought, every visualisation, every word spoken is speaking into existence which is energy work. The good news is when we witness this energy it becomes powerless and we can call back all the lost pieces.

2. Clearing It

The next step is to clear the energy from your aura and your partner if you relate to my situation and feel it's effecting your relationship - you could also do this with a friend if you feel your friendship has been effected. Acknowledging that this person has been sending you bad vibes is the first step. I would then encourage you to do an Angelic chord cutting meditation and verbally command their energy be sent back to them - that you now reclaim your power and all the lost pieces of you. This can be done firmly but it's also important to send this person on their loving healing path and ask that you are protected by light beings, Ascended Masters, Archangels or whatever resonates with you. One of the vampires I had to block and remove from my life, the other I had to offer up the relationship to the Universe and ask that this person change and up-level or they be removed from my life peacefully. Again all of this is positive energy work and it's important you don't tolerate this anymore. Standing in your power and not tolerating shit is the most powerful way to bust these vampires out of your life. If you do choose to keep this person in your life I would strongly suggest not sharing any vulnerable information with them, keep your emotions safe and protected as they will find a way back in if you let them. They are wanting to see you miserable so it's important you only share this sensitive information in a safe space around souls who will support and uplift you no matter what. To the vampires you simply say 'all is well' to them. I would also recommend getting some protective crystals such as clear quartz, black obsidian and black tourmaline. Call upon these crystals to protect you and shine light into your life again.

3. Shine Your Light

Once you feel this energy move through, you may experience a cold like me or an illness. Sorry to share but your body does flush out in all aspects - but this is good it's removing all the toxicity. Be really gentle with yourself after this process, honour and journal any emotions or triggers that do come up. You may need to rest or take a few days off and that is perfectly okay your body is purging and healing. This is all happening for your highest good and it will be a massive weight off your shoulders to release this energy and be in full control again.

4. Protect Yourself Daily

The next step is to protect yourself daily. I personally worked with an incredible soul called George Lizos, he taught me great ways to protect myself daily and I would highly recommend checking out his work on psychic attacks. The traditional way to protect yourself is to surround yourself with white light each morning, you can do this by calling in Archangel Michael and imagining a bright white bubble being formed around yourself. You can also carry around your protective crystals and use a cleansing or protective aura spray. George taught me some more advanced ways to protect myself daily which have also really helped - especially using essential oils. I was taken into a deep meditation where I was able to clear negative chords and I was told an essential oil to use by my spiritual guardian. I now use the essential oil every day and follow these energy clearing exercises religiously. You can also use these protection techniques for your online work which has helped me keep away any negativity.

The problem is sometimes we believe this low-level energy has power of us and it really doesn't, once again this is all an illusion. It's only when we believe this other person is more powerful that they gain power over us. So I would ask you to keep checking in with yourself and make sure you are speaking your truth and surrounded by light. I've always had people make claims against my success it's happened throughout my career these people get so bitter and jealous that they feel they are somehow responsible for my work and success. Silly I know as I barely know them!

The best thing I could do after this was acknowledge that no one has a right over my work only myself and I work god damn hard to be authentic and share my truth with the world. That is reflected in my success and you guys resonating with my work. The best thing I could do was heal and forgive these people, they were sent into my life (in the same month!) to teach me these life lessons and they were just doing their job. All you can do is send healing love and light and offer up this person to the Universe to determine whether they stay in your life and transform or walk away.

It's funny because I genuinely thought one day I'm going to have to explain to my love when he gets this, that I have literally been fighting a battle for us to be together! There was no logical explanation for our struggles, we had healed our wounds and up-levelled there was just no explanation for why it was all going well after the separation and then suddenly not again. I'm so grateful that I listened to my intuition and had an amazing soul like Hannah around me witness these bad energies. I know it may be hard to get your head around and we think but how is this possible?

It is simply through the other persons wounds and ego that they create these 'bad' stories about us and end up sending you bad vibes out of jealousy and anger. Yes these things happen but I want to remind you that there is a lot of love and light in this world - no matter what someone wants to send your way the Universe will always protect us from harm's way. When I had finally cleared this energy I felt like myself again, I no longer had these influences draining me or brainwashing me. I knew my truth once again - both peace and abundance started pouring in and once again everything started to go right in all areas of my life.

So to end this chapter I really want to talk about the light side of energy work and how powerful it can be. We all know that positive energy attracts positivity. So I would really invite you to create your own energy work ritual whether that's meditating, visualising, speaking into existence, writing letters can also be powerful too. There is no right or wrong answer. I also wrote love letters to my twin and asked that his higher self delivered them to him.

During the re-set of energy before this manifested into my reality, these practises were really powerful and allowed me to find peace and acceptance of our journey and know that the pain was over only happiness awaited us. As we up-level and shine in life some people aren't going to like it - our light will be a magnet to energies like this and personally being in the public eye doesn't help either. Luckily I know I'm protected online and know my work will only fall into the right people's hands. So although this all sounds like a dramatic battle for us to be together, I am so grateful this happened to encourage me to up-level, rise and own my truth. I was being called, against all odds, to believe in us, trust in my intuition, in the Universe and know that no matter what, love **always** wins.

Unstoppable Queen

As my final chapter in this book, I thought it was only fair that we looked back on the key points of Law of Attraction and create a master plan of how you can become unstoppable in the manifestation process. By now you should have some great tools and tricks to aid you in moments of uncertainty and fear. Your unlimited potential lies within you, if you can focus on your self-love, forgiving your past and most importantly letting go of your past, here lies your unlimited potential to manifest the life of your dreams.

This journey won't be easy unless you dedicate time each day to yourself and to your spiritual practises. I was able to manifest my entire dream life in under twelve months by fiercely committing to myself and manifestations. I allowed the Universe to direct me to the books I needed to read and the videos I had to film. Not only was I receiving this knowledge, I was equally sharing this knowledge with the world through my online content. Now I'm not saying you all need to start up a blog, but even if you just help a friend or give your old books to a stranger you're sharing your light into the world.

Releasing your fears, acknowledging them and transforming them will allow you to be fearless. Being fearless isn't anything to worry about, it's the ultimate vibration to be on to manifest continuously. When we accept the knowing that everything happens for a reason and that we are the authors of our life we become unstoppable. Even hiccups along the way become blessings in disguise and bring us even more rewarding lessons which is part of our soul mission.

By turning up each day to the Universe and being grateful, healing ourselves and sharing love into the world, we become a magnet for miracles. When we open up our awareness to miracles and cast our fear, we attract all forms of love and abundance into our lives.

I want you to dedicate the next twelve months of your life to you. I want you to get clear, get precise and get grounded in what you want to achieve by this time next year. I want you to follow these tips, exercises and practises in this book throughout the next year and fiercely dedicate each day to your manifestations and dream life. Start saying YASS to yourself, YASS to your life and YASS to your future because it's looking so magical and bright. The next year is in your hands, so why not make it a year to remember for all the right reasons? Using these pages or in a notebook, I want you to make a declaration today, date it and commit to this deceleration of love. I then want you to read it out loud in the mirror and then see it as done. Pull out this book or notebook in a year's time and see how much of this has come true and what an awesome abundant life you're now living. You've got this Queen, I believe in you!

Date -

I .... commit the next twelve months of my life to fiercely loving myself, my life and the Universe. I promise to work on myself, my self-love and always return to love when I have been led astray by fear based thoughts.

Over the next twelve months I will do my spiritual practises daily as this will help me to stay in alignment and in a high vibration to manifest. By this time next year I will have manifested...

_____

_____

_____

_____

_____

_____

_____

_____

_____

_____

I now bring these things to me or something else which is for my highest good. I can trust the Universe and I know these wonderful things will be brought to me at the right time and in the most perfect way. I release these manifestations now, knowing that the Universe has heard them and will deliver.

Over the next year I commit to healing my wounds, overcoming challenges with grace and positivity knowing that this is my soul mission. I say YASS to myself, YASS to my life, and YASS to my future because I have so many exciting and loving things to look forward to.

I .... am a Spiritual Queen and hold all the tools and techniques I need to manifest the life of my dreams. I am worthy and deserving of my manifestations and by manifesting these wonderful things into my life. I will also show those close to me how loving the Universe is so that when they are ready they too will lead happier and abundant lives.

And so it is...

"When you contact the Higher Self, the source of power within, you tap into a reservoir of infinite power."

—Deepak Chopra

Manifesting Queen

When I started writing this book I had no book deal, I wrote this book on faith knowing that by sharing my light in the world the Universe would arrange the rest for me. This book needed to be brought into the world and I trusted that. The journey I have been on since starting this book and attending that writers course has been incredible. The Universe has sent me on a journey of self-discovery, healing my own wounds and through this I was able to write this book with authenticity and with the help of the Universe.

The book deal didn't happen how I thought it would at all, but I know now looking back it was for my highest good. I followed my dream and got the most bizarre 'no' after months of being close to a book deal with one publisher. Normally, I would have been upset, thought it was me or the book who was a problem and put the book on hold thinking it was a sign to stop and wait until a better time. My intuition was screaming at me 'No this book is ready to go you have the green light it's perfect'. So I submitted my proposal to six other publishers and heard nothing.

Hannah my good friend suggested getting in touch with a new publisher called *That Guy's House*, after a phone call with Sean I knew my journey had been leading me to meeting him and his incredible company. Sean believed in my vision, he didn't want to change me, my brand or edit my voice. I knew I had found a like-minded soul who was doing great work in the world and I could trust. This journey has opened my eyes to the world of publishing, how hard it can be to be noticed even with my following and how some publishers want you to lose your voice and integrity just to sell books. This whole book was written on a journey of authenticity so to sell my truth for the sake of a book deal would have been all wrong. Signing my book deal with *That Guy's House* felt right and I knew that us working together would help so many people.

I'm proud to be a part of Sean's ever growing vision and I'm proud that this book has been birthed un-edited and raw. Just like all my work. It's almost ironic that I signed my book deal exactly a year to the week after starting this book on holiday in Santorini. So much has changed since that holiday. The journeys, battles and healing I've encountered have been life changing and this book is a diary of this transformation. I have transformed into the Queen I always knew I could be and have against all odds returned to love and risen above any obstacles.

We are all powerful Spiritual Queen's and together by sharing the light and showing up to our calling miracles happen. I wanted to document this journey with you to show you that the Universe works in mysterious ways. When it wants something to happen, nothing will stand in the way of a book, idea or creation reaching the people it needs to help. I've had a lot of rejections in my work which has always pushed me to find a way to do it myself. It has always been successful and has taught me that now a days we don't always have to go down the traditional routes to make our dreams happen.

I want to thank Sean for believing in me, my work and my purpose here because without him you guys wouldn't be reading this book. It's refreshing to see a new wave of publishers who do care about the message and don't want to edit our voices to fit into the mainstream publishing industry. I mean when have I ever fitted in!?

Anything is possible in this Universe and so many people over the years have tried to make claims on my couponing and spiritual work claiming they've put me where I am today. No, as you can tell I've done this all by myself, learning and adapting as I go. I am unique, my work is unique and as many times as people tried to put me down and tell me I'd never been an author. Did I listen to this NO! You don't need anyone's permission in this world to do you. Be fiercely, authentically and unapologetically you Queen because there is no one else like you out there! As we rise people will try and pull us back down to their level but just know you were never on their level anyway and you don't owe anyone anything. I spent years questioning why women backstab one another, why they can't be happy for others doing well when I'm the first one to cheer when I see any woman owning her body, truth, voice or passion. I believe there are fantastic women doing wonders in the world and we can get to a place where we all love and accept one another.

Over the last five years as I've awakened and gone through frankly life shaping experiences, I've realised I played small for far too long. I'm sure you can all relate to this too, we're so worried about fitting in and conforming to these conditioning behaviours that we forget how to be us. So what we burn things on a full moon, so what we wear crystals, so what we manifest incredible things into our life.

We are incredible light beings with a purpose here on this earth to return to love and be one with all that is. Some people won't get that and that's okay just know that it has no reflection on you and you should shine your light regardless. I chose some tough lessons to learn very early on in my life and these have shaped me into the woman you see today. Yes it has been tough, yes I have screamed at the Universe sometimes thinking 'Why is this happening to me when I share so much light into the world and turn up every day?' the truth is this is exactly what I'm meant to be doing. I chose this path to grow rapidly and inspire others to do the same and live their best life. There was no easy way around this apart from learning these lessons myself.

As I finish writing this book I'm tuning twenty-five and as I reflect on the last year of my life which has been writing this book, I see the growth, strength and courage I've had to provide myself to continue showing up and move through the struggles, challenges and battles you've witnessed in this book. Over the last year the real lessons I've learnt is how much strength one person can have. I'm not saying my experiences have crippled me because I know there are a lot worse things that can happen to someone so I do feel blessed to some extent that the lessons have simply been emotional but it's all relevant to the individual anyway. I know the Universe has always stood by me and I've been able to connect to myself, my purpose and the Universe further. Through my darkest days I wrote this book, although my dark night of the soul seems years ago now I still went through an awakening due to the twin flame process and karmic reasonings. Throughout this all I've showed up every day, to you, for myself and for the Universe. This is what I believe the meaning of real strength is that against all odds I chose love and peace.

I know some of you reading this will want to share your experiences too, whether that be in a group of friends or on a stage to thousands of people. More voices are being heard and I love this. We can use the power of technology and social media to reach more people, connect and share more light into the world. I myself love social media it has been a massive strength of mine and has certainly helped transform my passions into successful profitable businesses. So I encourage anyone reading this no matter your circumstances use this book as the spiritual sign you need to start living your best life today and being the badass Spiritual Queen I know you can be.

Stop listening to others who tell you opposite, stop listening to the people who aren't even helping themselves. We only get one shot at this lifetime and this life is way too short to play small, to tolerate bullshit, to listen to the doubters or to no be doing what you love right now. We all want that freedom whether it be financially or emotionally and we can have both, we can create meaningful lives that make a positive impact in the world. That all starts within you, nurture and worship yourself give yourself the love and support you need right now. When you come from a place of love and peace the whole game changes.

Through my manifesting journey I've come to realise that while the Universe does provide us with all that we ask for both good and bad because it is simply responding to our vibration. It also provides us with so much more, it provides us with this journey and this opportunity to up-level and not only have incredible manifestations in our life but the chance to share this joy with the world.

Imagine if everyone who read this book or knew about the Law of Attraction went and shared this with one friend, shared the concept and what happiness it has brought them. Without fear of judgement or rejection, if that one friend changed their life and then passed it on to another. This is what I've always tried to implement on my channels and in my personal life. Although some have been hesitant, eventually when they see how much positivity and light it has brought into my life and my work they can't deny it anymore.

The key is to hand someone the information and let them make an informed decision as to what they connect with. If each of us did this think of the magnitude of love and positivity that would start to radiate out in the world. This is certainly already happening and fast, but if we can consciously make an effort to share this message through your business, work, friend groups, family, relationships, strangers think about the mass healing and peace that would occur. Your task here on this earth is to one heal and live your best life but secondly to share this light with others. So if you are in unfulfilling situations right now, whether that be relationships or career, you can change this. Be the change you want to see in the world, when you start voicing your truth and living your authentic life your whole world will have to reflect this too.

Since doing this in my own life my friends, family and partner have all done this themselves they are finding the light which means collectively if we show up, they show up too. So no more excuses, start that business you've been meaning to start, quit that job that bores you, remove the energy vampires from your life, start manifesting your dream love, book that holiday - stop standing in the way of abundance and happiness that is awaiting you. Sometimes we get comfortable playing small because it's what we know and we fear we'll be judged or loose people. Queen, if people leave your life because you up-level and are happy they were never meant for you! You deserve the best kind of people in your life who grow with you and support you no matter what.

If you've wanted to qualify in something now is your time, if you want to write a book like I have - do it! I didn't have a publisher when I started I just answered the call the Universe sent my way and the rest fell into place at the right time. Maybe it's an e-book, a course to help people all of this whether it's spiritual or not is answering your call and showing up each day. When we put off these callings in life and play small the Universe has to hit us with what I like to call a life truck. When we don't answer these calls and step out of our comfort zone sometimes we have to quite literally be knocked onto the right path where we simply can't ignore it anymore. We chose our soul missions so ask yourself what is your purpose here? Are you fulfilling your soul's calling? If not what can you do today to change this?

If you are unsure of what your purpose could be really tune into your intuition, ask your spirit guides to show you through synchronicities. You can connect to your spirit guides purely through intention. Ask them to start showing you signs, ask them what their names are and listen for an answer. The more you trust the information that is coming to you the stronger the connection grows and you will be able to communicate clearly with them.

Trust the names that come to you and look out for the signs. The answers will come when you open up to them. I hope this book has allowed you to see that playing small only works for so long and if you are like me and are here to achieve big things you are going to need to answer that call and say 'I'm ready!'. So whatever it is you've been putting off it's time to own it and claim your power. Take charge of your destiny and become accepting of the knowledge that you can have anything you desire in this Universe. You are worthy and deserving of all life has to offer and the fact you are reading this book means something. That you've been called to spirituality, this way of life which can literally transform every single aspect into love and happiness.

All you have to do is answer the call and show up every single day, for yourself, for the universe and for others. If you can walk away with one thing from this book I hope that it is motivation and inspiration to live your best life now without limitation. I so hope my journey has shown you that anything can be achieved and that the Universe can move mountains to ensure our voices are heard. I hope you can take away tools, resources and information that will continue to serve you and aid you in healing and manifesting your dream life. Over anything else the one key lesson I've learnt in this process is that *love always wins* so as long as we speak our truth and show up only good will follow.

The future looks bright for us all, but personally I am excited to embark on the next chapter of my life with my love and career. I'm excited for the clients I will help, the books I will write, the events I will hold all with the vision of meeting as many of you as possible and having one big party to celebrate life with you. Life is magical and magic can be found in even the strangest of places. If only we could all have that childlike imagination again where we believed pure magic was all around us. The truth is the magic never left us we just grew up...

"And above all, watch with glittering eyes the whole world around you because the greatest secrets are always hidden in the most unlikely places. Those who don't believe in magic will never find it."

—Roald Dahl

Acknowledgements

I first of all want to thank you all for reading this book, without you this dream wouldn't be possible. I want to thank my best friend, twin flame and partner Grant for being my biggest teacher and inspiration in life without even knowing it. Also, my family and friends for holding the space for me to be myself, to explore my spirituality and for being my biggest cheerleaders.

I want to thank Yasmin Boland for being an inspiration to me and guiding me through my Author journey. Your kind and honest words mean the world to me. I also want to thank my biggest inspirations Gabrielle Bernstein, Rebecca Campbell, Kyle Gray and Tony Robbins for showing up to their calling and inspiring me to follow mine. Not only has your worked inspired me it will inspire so many millions more.

I want to thank every single soul and teacher that has touched my life in some way, because you shaped the person I am today and I am forever grateful for the lessons you've taught me. Without these experiences I wouldn't be able to be authentic and raw in my own teachings.

I want to thank you my readers because you have listened to the Universe, awoken to your calling and are now changing your life, now that's a miracle and the biggest compliment I could ever receive. This book is the beginning of my work, I am proud of how far I've come and how much I've grown throughout this book. Through writing these chapters I've become the Spiritual Queen I always knew I could be. So thank you for reading this, thank you for being you and thank you for always supporting my work and allowing me to shine my light.

Recommendations

BOOKS

Light Is The New Black - Rebecca Campbell

Raise Your Vibration - Kyle Gray

A Return To Love - Marianne Williamson

A Course In Miracles - Helen Schucman

The Universe Has Your Back - Gabrielle Bernstein

The Magic - Rhonda Bryne

You Can Heal Your Life - Louise Hay

Moonology - Yasmin Boland

VIDEOS

Brad Yates (Youtube Channel) EFT - Emotional Freedom Technique

Yoga with Adriene (Youtube Channel)

RESOURCES

Manifestation Mediation Playlist - Emma Mumford

www.emmamumford.co.uk (shop)

Law of Attraction Development Course - Emma Mumford

Rachel Rendell - Psychic - www.rachelrendell.co.uk

About The Author

Emma Mumford is an award-winning lifestyle Blogger, YouTuber, Life Coach, Reiki Master, Public Speaker, Author and regular on ITV's This Morning. Emma also hosts the popular Podcast 'Spiritual Queen's Badass Podcast' available on iTunes & Acast. Emma also has her own Law of Attraction merchandise range available on her website shop and Etsy store. Emma also holds monthly webinars over on her website and has numerous free resources across her website and social media channels for you to explore.

Emma started her savvy savings journey back in 2013. After finding Couponing in her hour of need thanks to her ex-partner leaving her with his £7k debt – Emma then set up the nationally popular brand Extreme Couponing and Deals UK LTD and became known as the UK's Coupon Queen. In 2016, Emma underwent a spiritual awakening and knew that her calling in life was to move away from her money-saving roots and grow into the personal development world with her own brand.

| **www.emmamumford.co.uk** |

| **@iamemmamumford** |

Lightning Source UK Ltd.
Milton Keynes UK
UKHW011829070119
335148UK00009B/587/P

9 781912 779413